DELHI RIOTS 2020
THE UNTOLD STORY

MONIKA ARORA

SONALI CHITALKAR   PRERNA MALHOTRA

गरुड

Published by
Garuda Prakashan Private Limited
Gurugram, Bharat

www.garudabooks.com

First published in India 2020

ISBN: 9781942426295

Cover Design: Rohit Bawne

CONTENTS

MESSAGE

Delhi Riots 2020: The Untold Story, is a serious document of intense research. It is the result of the painstaking efforts of visiting ground zero of these communal riots and hotspots by the spirited citizens of the Group of Intellectuals and Academicians (GIA). I have read the book thoroughly. It was very engaging and extremely informative. One really gets unnerved about the kinds of plans that are afoot to break up the country.

India will have to reckon with a huge challenge from the Urban Naxals and fundamentalist Islamic groups. It will be a long haul and the nation has to be prepared for it. The Urban Naxals/Marxists-Leninists believe in breaking India into small independent nations—this also suits global powers The idea is to form an alliance with religious fundamentalists and to form a formidable 'break-India' gang.

So, as a nation, India will have to be well prepared at all times to combat the toxin being spread by these break-India forces, backed by certain political elements. I congratulate GIA for making this stupendous effort to bring these facts to light.

Sh. P C Dogra IPS (Retd)
Former Director General of Police, Punjab
Chandigarh

FOREWORD

Throughout history, colonizers have attacked the world's indigenous peoples and civilizations, and sought to erase and write over their culture and knowledge. The library of Alexandria at the temple at Serapeum in Egypt was burnt by Theophilus, the bishop of Alexandria, in a zeal to wipe out paganism. In the Spanish conquest of the Yucatan peninsula, thousands of Mayan codices were burnt by the Bishop Diego de Landa, claiming they were superstitions from the devil, eviscerating Mayan knowledge. Only four codices survived.

Successfully colonizing a people necessitates undermining their histories and knowledge and rewriting them to the colonizer's advantage. India was subject to colonization by two world-dominant religions. The Turkic-Mughal conquest burnt down universities, libraries and temples, all of which were sites of knowledge production and dissemination. The British conquest colonized by rewriting Indian histories and fabricating narratives and theories. Indigenous education and knowledge systems were destroyed and new ones, which suited the colonizer, were set up. These universities and institutions, and the intellectuals they produced and heralded, were established to perpetuate the colonial gaze. It is a long journey to undo this intellectual coloniality—institutional control of the narrative through production, publishing and distribution of knowledge remains.

At the same time, a host of Indians trained in these institutions continue to "interpret" India for the West, often at the behest of powerful global groupings. They retrofit India into ill-fitting European epistemes. For instance, "minority" in the US or Europe refers to non-White or non-Christian people who have been systemically disenfranchised in empirically demonstrable ways. In India, the term "minority" refers simply to the demographic minorities within the population, communities which belong to the two world-dominant religions which also colonized India, rather than coming from a history of systemic disenfranchisement. The intellectual dishonesty in conflating these two definitions of "minority" is glaring. These master narratives engage unethical conflations to misrepresent the continued violence in India of the globally dominant and well-resourced powerful groupings against the Hindu population they previously colonized.

Similarly, reference to the "Left" in India is not about some socialist center-Left policies. "Socialist" is part of the preamble of the Indian Constitution and all parties, including the so-called "right-wing" BJP, aver by it. The Indian Left are self-avowed Communist parties. Radical Left groups are responsible for more terrorism in India than any other ideological grouping. According to the Global Terrorism Index[1], "The deadliest group in India is the country's communist party—The Communist Party of India (Maoists). Maoists were responsible for 205 deaths and 190 terror incidents in India, or 53 per cent of deaths in 2017." These groups, also known as Naxals, have logistical support and intellectual covering fire from urban centers and universities, and these are termed Urban Naxals[2].

The top four global terror groups per the Global Terrorism Index are Islamic[1]. A combination of Urban Naxals and Islamic radicalism is a deadly cocktail, as the events described in the book attest. These radical elements are not even amenable to intervention from Muslim clerics who are part of India's plural tapestry. According to the authors, Maulana Mohammad Daud Amini and Maulana Mohammad Shamim were themselves attacked and castigated as they appealed to the mob to abjure violence and clear the roads they were blocking.

This book was to be published by Bloomsbury India, a subsidiary of Bloomsbury UK, which had approved the content. Very close to the launch, Bloomsbury India pulled the book, apparently on orders of headquarters at Bloomsbury UK. This was egged on by a White male organizer of a major literary festival in India to shut down the voices of the three Indian women authors. A definitive act of colonial White privilege.

The authors turned to Garuda, a publishing house with an explicit aim of decolonization. Stars aligned and magic happened. Indians stood up to be counted. Within 24 hours of pre-launch, over 15,000 copies were pre-sold on the garudabooks.com website. People were hungry for authentic stories and tired of colonial gatekeepers determining who has permission to write, and what they get to read.

It was a sign of the emerging shoots of new India, one which will not be held back, though it is demonized via the academic and global narrative. It is a cry for a plural world where multiple viewpoints are given space rather than pre-judged and de-platformed by dominant forces. More perspectives on the tragic events in Delhi in 2019-2020 should be welcomed, as talking with each other rather than past each other, is the way forward for a plural society.

Sankrant Sanu

Author, "The English Medium Myth" and CEO Garuda Prakashan

References
1. Global Terrorism Index 2018, compiled by the Institute for Economics & Peace (IEP). http://visionofhumanity.org/app/uploads/2018/12/Global-Terrorism-Index-2018-1.pdf
2. Agnihotri, Vivek, Urban Naxals. Garuda Prakashan, 2018. https://www.garudabooks.com/urbannaxals

PREFACE

As we bring forth this publication based on the ground report of the Delhi Riots early this year, which was a fact-finding mission undertaken by the Group of Intellectuals and Academicians (GIA) I am filled with a sense of having fulfilled our moral duty. After multiple visits to North East Delhi in the aftermath of the riots in February 2020, it was incumbent upon us to tell the world the true story of the agony faced by the 53 victims who lost their lives in this senseless violence. I am also aware that telling their story and that of the ordinary people who suffered economic losses and faced the naked terror on the streets of Delhi is necessary to cut through the rhetoric and propaganda associated with this episode of engineered communal violence. GIA watched with concern as Delhi burnt on 23–26 February 2020. However much before the immediate violence, members of the GIA discussed and worried over the deepening stress and tension that was being deliberately created in our beloved city over the Citizenship Amendment Act (CAA). Some of our members, who teach in various colleges in Delhi University (DU) and Jawaharlal Nehru University (JNU), noted the deliberate escalation of communal fault lines in Delhi at anti-CAA protest sites. We visited Shaheen Bagh to understand the happenings on the ground. And we came back appalled at the senseless dramatics being orchestrated by random groups there. We saw first-hand how theatrics and ideology, cloaked under the banner of the Tricolour and the Indian Constitution, barely hid a communal undertone. It was here that Kali, the free and fierce Hindu goddess, was imprisoned in a hijab. It was in Shaheen Bagh that Aum and the Swastika, holy to all Indic faiths, were desecrated.

As members of the public, we faced the circumstances created at protest sites, just like all the common citizens of this city were facing daily. We faced traffic jams due to the Shaheen Bagh blockage, at times Metro services were suddenly suspended due to disruptions by anti-CAA protesters. Getting home from work was a frustrating prospect. We saw how our democracy was rendered helpless by law enforcement and a legal system that was working to accommodate the right to protest. We witnessed the systematic blocking of arterial roads in Delhi at multiple locations. These blockages were designed to cut off populations and isolate potentially combustible areas of Delhi. We saw as crowds of protesters stormed the marketplaces in our vicinity and chose to stand in front of Hindu places of worship to raise azadi slogans. We felt the terror as protesters slammed the gates of our homes while raising slogans for the freedom of Kashmir. However, nothing prepared us for the violent hate unleashed on common citizens from the anti-CAA protest sites in North East Delhi.

GIA went to North East Delhi from 29 February 2020 onwards and made multiple visits to gather data till the submission of the report to the minister of state for home (MoS [Home]) Shri G. Kishan Reddy on 11 March 2020. We had held extensive interviews with victims, residents of these areas and law-enforcement personnel. We met religious leaders from both communities who worked to de-escalate the situation. The GIA ground report was an outcome of intense research and data gathering from violence-affected areas in North East Delhi.

I am thankful to Professor Vijita S. Aggarwal for her invaluable support in finalising this book. Divyansha Sharma has been a constant support for media and technical expertise.

I dedicate this book to all the victims of the Delhi riots in North East Delhi. Many young and promising lives were cut short by the bullets of hate that flew unrestrained in the area. Amongst the many victims were members of the Scheduled Caste communities who were brutalised in unimaginable ways. The weaker sections of society, like the nomads in Khajuri Khas, were also victims of the violence.

Nothing that we write or say can convey the depth of the tragedy of these riots. This book is an attempt to bring out the true story of the Delhi Riots. It is a call for remembering that communal fault lines were created between neighbours by ideologically vested interests comprising Urban Naxals and Jihadi elements who had an agenda to implement—to systematically conflagrate areas with mixed populations of Hindus and Muslims and take these areas from dharna to danga.

The insidious mindset of the Urban Naxals and Jihadis led to the creation and execution of the dharna-to-danga model in Delhi. This book is an attempt to tell the fact- and evidence-based story of this model that the GIA's fact-finding team gathered from North East Delhi.

Advocate Monika Arora
Convener, GIA

LIST OF ABBREVATIONS

- Akhil Bharatiya Vidyarthi Parishad (ABVP)
- Aligarh Muslim University (AMU)
- All-India Majlis-e-Ittahadul Muslimeen (AIMIM)
- All-India Students' Association (AISA)
- Assistant Commissioner of Police (ACP)
- Bharatiya Janata Party (BJP)
- Birsa Ambedkar Phule Students' Association (BAPSA)
- Chhatra Yuva Sangharsh Samiti (CYSS)
- Chief Justice of India (CJI)
- Citizenship Amendment Act (CAA)
- Code of Criminal Procedure (CrPC)
- Communist Party of India, Maoist (CPI [M])
- Delhi Noida Direct (DND)
- Deputy Commissioner of Police (DCP)
- Electronic Voting Machines (EVMs)
- Enforcement Directorate (ED)
- Film and Television Institute of India (FTII)
- First Information Report (FIR)
- Fourth Generation Warfare (4GW)
- Grant Trunk Karnal Road (GT Karnal)
- Group of Intellectuals and Academicians (GIA)
- Guru Teg Bahadur (GTB) Hospital
- Indian Institute of Technology (IIT)
- Indian Mujahideen (IM)
- Indian National Congress (INC)
- Indian Penal Code (IPC)
- Intelligence Bureau (IB)
- Islamic State for Syria and Iraq (ISIS)

- Jamaat-e-Islami (JeI)
- Jamia Millia Islamia (JMI)
- Jawaharlal Nehru University (JNU)
- JNU Students' Union (JNUSU)
- Karnataka Forum for Dignity (KFD)
- Left Democratic Front (LDF)
- Left-Wing Extremists (LWE)
- Manitha Neethi Pasarai (MNP)
- Maoist Communist Centre (MCC)
- Member of the Legislative Assembly (MLA)
- Minister of State (MoS)
- Municipal Corporation of Delhi (MCD)
- National Commission for Protection of Child Rights (NCPCR)
- National Democratic Alliance (NDA)
- National Development Front (NDF)
- National Human Rights Commission (NHRC)
- National Investigation Agency (NIA)
- National Population Register (NPR)
- National Register for Citizens (NRC)
- Peoples' Democratic Party (PDP) of Kerala
- Peoples' War Group (PWG)
- Popular Front of India (PFI)
- Prevention of Terrorism Act (POTA)
- Railway Protection Force (RPF)
- Rapid Action Force (RAF)
- Rashtriya Janta Dal (RJD)
- Rashtriya Swayamsevak Sangh (RSS)
- Residents' Welfare Association (RWA)
- Social Democratic Party of India (SDPI)
- Station House Officer (SHO)
- Student's Islamic Organisation (SIO)
- Students Islamic Movement of India (SIMI)
- Students' Federation of India (SFI)
- United Democratic Front (UDF)
- Uttar Pradesh (UP)

ONE

INTRODUCTION

हो गयी है पीर पर्वत सी...

– दुष्यंत कुमार

Delhi, the city of kings and emperors, is an intrigue, a mystery, a grand story of continuous inhabitation since prehistoric times. The city has been built many times over. The ruins of at least eight capitals have been discovered in Delhi. Indraprastha[1], the city of the Pandavas mentioned in the Mahabharata, is said to have been situated in Delhi around 3500 BC. Anecdotal evidence points to the Purana Qila built on the site of Indraprastha. Some archaeological evidence (the presence of ancient Indian pottery such as Northern Black Polished Ware and Painted Grey Ware also points to the area being inhabited as early as 1000 BCE. Further, according to some sources, the city of Delhi was founded by one Raja Dhilu around 800 BCE.[1]

Though there is limited historical evidence about the natives of Delhi, it is widely believed that the Tomars were settled along the Yamuna river basin and their founder, Anangapala, established Delhi in 736 AD. The Tomar clan lived and intermixed with Rajputs, Gurjars and Jats.

In the 12th century, the Chauhans (the Rajput dynasty to which the legendary Prithviraj Chauhan belonged) took over from the Tomars. Then came the Muslims from Afghanistan, Central Asia and Iran who built Siri, Tughlaqabad, Firozabad, Shahjahanabad, which are all encompassed in Delhi. This period saw many dynasties and sultanates from 1206 to 1526 AD, Delhi was ruled successively by the Slave Dynasty (1206–1290); the Khilji Dynasty (1290–1320); the Tughlaq Dynasty (1320–1413); the Sayyid Dynasty (1414–1451); the Lodi Dynasty (1451–1526) and the Mughals (1526–1761).

Though technically, the Mughal rulers continued to exist right up to 1857, the Mughal rule, however, was significantly weakened after 1757, when the Marathas captured Delhi and enforced their writ on the Mughal emperor, Alamgir II. The Marathas, however, lost this control to East India Company in 1803. Undoubtedly, this grand political history was supported by the simple, warm and welcoming population of the Yamuna basin. Many people from the Kayastha community from Uttar Pradesh (UP) moved to Delhi during the Mughal reign to work as administrators in their courts.

The Civil Lines area in Delhi was settled by British residents from the 19th century right up to the time when they built New Delhi (1911–1931). This is evident in the architecture that can be seen in Civil Lines, which reflects the colonial styles that were popular at the time. Many Bengalis, mostly officers in the administration made a move to Delhi in 1911 as the capital of the British Empire in India was shifted from Calcutta. They took up residence around the Gole Market area. (In 1971, many moved to Chittaranjan Park, where the East Pakistan Displaced Persons Colony were established after the second war with Pakistan) The 1947 Partition witnessed a flood of Punjabi and some Sindhi refugees into Delhi, which earned it the tag of 'Punjabi City'. Many areas of Delhi like Patel Nagar still carry the stamp of this exodus.

In 1990, the exodus of the Kashmiri Pandits from what is now the erstwhile state of Jammu and Kashmir saw them moving to areas like Vasant Kunj. Delhi welcomed Tibetan refugees as they fled from Chinese occupation. The Tibetan refugees made a life in the city, settling in North Delhi in the Majnu Ka Tilla neighbourhood. A walk through these lanes will transport one to Lhasa. The last 20 years have seen a huge influx of people from Bihar and UP, and people from northern hill states living in East Delhi. Then there are labourers from Rajasthan and Odisha who are spread all over. People from the Northeast have also moved to Delhi in large numbers in the last two decades.[2] People from Kerala and Tamil Nadu also form significant communities. A large population of Sri Lankan Tamils have made their homes in narrow lanes of Janakpuri. Delhi also continues to be an important centre for students all over the country.

Further, being the seat of the central government, as well as having seen the emergence of large corporate hubs in Delhi itself along with neighbouring Gurugram and Noida, Delhi and its contiguous urban setting is home to not only people from all over India but also a large number of expatriates from all over the world.

This melting pot of people has seen a huge churning in its way of being, thoughts, cuisine, culture and attitudes. It will be fair to say that today's Delhi is the result of all this churn and while particular influences can be seen in different parts of the city, on the whole, Delhi can be seen as a teeming metropolis of mixed influences. The city is also a rapidly growing metropolitan area. According to details from the 2011 census, Delhi has a population of 1.68 crore, an increase from the 2001 census figure of 1.39 crore. The population of Delhi continues to rise rapidly and it is quite likely that the 2021 census, the population will have crossed two crore. If the contiguous metropolitan areas in Uttar Pradesh and Haryana were to be included, it will be much larger.

Delhi has seen communal violence in the past, some of the worst incidents in 1947. In 1984, Delhi saw the Sikh riots, which were 'retributory' political violence by the ruling party against a minority community in the aftermath of the assassination of Prime Minister Indira Gandhi.

The latest in the series are the violent communal clashes that occurred in North East Delhi, from 23 to 25 February

2020. Predictably, the national and international media also erupted in a frenzy of reporting and documentation of the riots. In today's social-media-controlled context of the rapid spread of news, horrific images of the violence were being broadcast. Video feeds of people fleeing burning public installations went viral, leading to a rapidly escalating communal situation. The situation prompted GIA to make a ground assessment of the situation. This book is based on that ground report of this riot.

Delhi Riots 2020: Not Riots But a First-of-Its-Kind Urban Warfare in India

Like any other country in the world, India has had a long history of intermittent sectarian riots in pre- and post-independent periods, wherein one section/group of society used violence against the other with whatever weapon was at hand—bricks, stones, rods, sticks, swords, etc. However, the violence which has happened in North East Delhi on 23–25 February 2020 is unprecedented in the rioting history of this country and cannot be just classified as a riot. It is a pre-planned systematic conspiracy, complete urban warfare, the first episode of its kind in India, engineered by radical Muslims and Urban Maoists in tandem.

There is a lot of evidence to prove that the Shaheen Bagh protest and rioting model was not spontaneous, triggered by some instigation as it happens in most cases of rioting. It was pre-planned warfare in which the militant Islamic organization Popular Front of India (PFI) played a pivotal role, with support of left-wing extremist (LWE) organizations. Islamic radicals have been at the forefront in protests and rioting whereas the Leftist role has been subtle and tactical. Select academics and media persons have not only been providing a shield to the violence but supporting it even by creating a wider narrative in their favour through their established presence in the national and international media. This technique of the Left to use Muslims as their striking arm is not new though and is something they have been doing since the 1940s.[3]

The Background to the Protests and Rioting: The Old Fault Line of Indian Society Exploited

Insecurities of the Muslims were exploited in the Shaheen Bagh protest and rioting model. Some of the developments at the level of the executive and the judiciary in the past few months had caused uneasiness in the Muslim community. A strong decision was taken by the Modi government to resolve long-pending issues of the Jammu and Kashmir region by setting aside Article 370 and bringing the area at par with other regions of the country. Then, the government at the Centre took yet another decision of doing away with instant triple talaq. The Supreme Court of India too resolved the decades-long cases related to the Ram Janmabhoomi issue and the verdict came in favour of considering the plot of land under dispute as the birthplace of Lord Ram. Then, on 11 December 2019, the government passed the Citizenship Amendment Act (CAA), to fast-track some time-bound cases of citizenship of six minority communities from three neighbouring countries.

The CAA had nothing to do with the Muslims of India. However, the Left grabbed this opportunity to exploit the fear of some Muslims. It misused the uneasiness brewing in the Muslim community for some months, ever since the BJP came to power again with a bigger mandate after the 2019 Lok Sabha elections. This, it did with some tacit support of a few political parties with vested interests.

A completely fake narrative was created by the Left in the national and international media and Indian universities regarding the CAA. Muslims were radicalised over more than two months at these anti-CAA protest sites. Details of this systematic, engineered radicalisation and outright confrontationist identity politics are given the subsequent chapters of this book. Women and children were used to feed venom against Hindus, the government, the security forces and the country at large. The Shaheen Bagh protest and violence model was devised, which innocently got support from some neutral apolitical citizens of Delhi too. Meanwhile, the funding links between the protests and the riots have been established to the PFI. The increasing influence of the PFI in some areas has already been pointed out and is being investigated by the National Investigation Agency (NIA) and covered by the media. PFI is allegedly working as a recruitment and training front for the global terrorist group, the Islamic State in Syria and Iraq, better known as ISIS. The Left and PFI have also been working closely in Kerala for the past several years, with both organisations having built and strengthened their presence in the southern state.

First-of-Its-Kind Strategy Adopted in Anti-CAA Protests and Rioting

The strategy and tactics followed in the Delhi protests and riots are the first of its kind in India, whereas they have frequently been used in Syria and other troubled areas of Middle East—specifically in Iraq on American forces.

The Shaheen Bagh Model, from protest to rioting, is a complete experiment. Incidents that took place from 15 December 2019 to 25 February 2020 are strategic phases of one plan.

The protest at Shaheen Bagh was used as a diversionary technique. While the media and police focused on the street protests, rioting structures were being identified and created in high-rise buildings in the other part of Delhi. This is a typical tactic applied in Maoist-infested forest areas of central India. 'Shout in the East and Strike in the West' has been the Maoist strategy wherein they create some movement at one place and strike at some other place. It is a part of the Guerrilla warfare tactics.

With such elaborate preparations, high-rises were used by snipers in North East Delhi during riots. North East Delhi's Rajdhani Public School in Shiv Vihar, Khajuri Khas was used by Muslim rioters as a base for storing weaponry and launching petrol and acid bombs, and bricks and stones through catapults. Similarly, the house of Tahir Hussain, an Aam Admi Party (AAP) councillor which is a huge building was used as a bunker and launch pad. The Intelligence Bureau (IB) officer, Ankit Sharma was allegedly stabbed to death and tortured for hours in the same building.

Hate speeches and sustained political mobilisation around CAA in the anti-CAA dharna sites had already created a situation of public violence on the streets since December 2019. The blocking of Road Number 66 in Jaffrabad on the night of 22 February 2020 provided the immediate cause of riots which began by the afternoon of 23 February 2020. The fact is that tons of acid pouches, a large quantity of stones and bricks and petrol were present in the areas which were accumulated over some weeks at least. Moreover, permanent slingshots and catapults were created through welding to target identified persons and locations. That is proof in itself that the targets were already set as the catapults' angles and directions were fixed. There are possibilities that PFI or ISI might have provided the lists of targeted individuals as most of the targets of Islamic snipers were individuals who either belonged to security forces—police, intelligence agencies or persons belonging to Hindu organisations.

Trained professional shooters were present in these buildings demarcated as bases to launch attacks. They could accurately shoot from a distance of around 300 metres, killing targets by aiming for the head or neck. Intelligence agencies need to investigate who provided such trained sharpshooters. Based on some of the bullets that were recovered by the investigating team, the use of sniper rifles was evident.

A supply chain through strong iron chains was created for rioters at the Rajdhani School building. The use of such tactics is not possible without combat training. Owned by a prominent Muslim local, Faisal Farroque, the wall of the Rajdhani Public School overlooks the D.R.P. Convent Public School in Shiv Vihar. While the latter was a single storey building, the former is a high-rise. Iron chains were suspended from the roof of the Rajdhani school and rioters rappelled their way into D.R.P., which was razed to the ground and burnt.

The use of women as shields is a typical Communist technique adopted over the years in the Left-dominated universities and at most of the protests. In all other previous protests and riots involving the Muslim community, women were sent to safer places while the men were part of the action. However, at Shaheen Bagh, women and children came on the forefront while the men made all the background preparations for rioting.

The fact that different types of weapons were gathered, from stones, bricks, sticks and rods to pistols and rifles, speaks about the systematic use of diverse weapons.

The brutal killing of Ankit Sharma with more than 51 wounds on his body is indicative of ISIS type of killings.

The police force has been a target of such forces on previous occasions, but targeting an intelligence officer is a big message which was communicated to create fear.

Finally, the timing of the riots was crucial as well, with the president of the United States, Donald Trump on a visit to India at the time. The likely motive was to internationalise the issue of Muslim unrest when the international media was all around and build a fake narrative against the current Indian government.

The Shaheen Bagh Protest and Rioting Model Is Just a Prelude

The Delhi protest and violence model is a kind of trailer of an unprecedented experiment in Delhi, the headquarters of the IB. It will be analysed not only by intelligence and law enforcement agencies but by the planners and executors of this model too. Never in the history of India have riots been planned and executed in such a systematic way. There is a pre-planned structure to this experiment which could further be applied to other Muslim-dominated areas of the country. This experiment could be a prelude to more such types of urban warfare in the future.

The responsibility of the central government is huge in the present circumstances, as the intelligence agencies and law enforcement agencies are under its direct control. Drastic steps need to be taken to strengthen intelligence as it is the first line of defence. Technology is important but there is no alternative to grass-root level human interaction. The NIA has the mandate to look into such systematic terror activities. Therefore, the investigation of the Delhi riots should be handed over to NIA for a fair probe. Moreover, the government cannot afford to neglect Delhi bureaucratically, politically and strategically and not strengthen itself in institutions of significance.

The deadly concoction of Jihadi elements and Urban Naxals is horrible and poisonous for the country. Both have inherited a long history of violence. Both have helped each other in the past but now both of them have started inheriting each other's strengths in terms of capability to launch violence and unrest. The numbers of the radicalised militant Muslims with logistical and tactical support of Left can prove dangerous in the times to come. This joint venture of radical Islam and the Left will destroy the country if it is not contained now. The tremendous social polarisation happening at their combined behest needs to be stopped to save the country from big losses of lives and property, in addition to other long-term socio-political, economic and psychological impacts.

So that We Never See This Again: Insights and Way Forward

The Delhi riots, which lasted for two-and-a-half days, roughly from 23 February 2020 afternoon to the night of 25 February 2020, have scarred the consciousness of the city. Now is the time for all of us to take stock and pledge that this sort of barbarous brutality never occurs again. To do that, we have to go into the reasons for this outbreak. The reasons enumerated in the following chapters are the ones we gathered from ground zero.

References

1. Chopra, Prabha. 1976. *Delhi Gazetteers*, p. 41. New Delhi: Publications Division, Ministry of Information and Broadcasting.
2. McDuie-Ra, Duncan. 2012. *Northeast Migrants in Delhi: Race, Refuge and Retail*. Amsterdam: Amsterdam University Press.
3. Ahmed, Ishtiaq. 2015. How far left of Partition? https://www.thefridaytimes.com/how-far-left-of-partition/, downloaded on 22 May 2020

TWO

THE THEORY OF URBAN NAXALISM AND JIHADISM

It would not be an exaggeration to say that the problem of Naxalism is the single biggest internal security challenge ever faced by our country.

– Dr. Manmohan Singh, Prime Minister of India, 2006

Introduction

The Delhi riots show clear indications that the Urban Naxal–Jihadi model has been applied in North East Delhi to create communal violence. They experimented with this model at all sites of the anti-CAA protests in the country. The model, however, succeeded in select places where there is a concentration of Urban Naxal and Jihadi elements, primarily in urban areas. This chapter explains the theoretical basis of Urban Naxalism and Jihad. The primary sources used to explain these models are source documents periodically disseminated by the Communist Party of India, Maoist (CPI [M]), the Jamaat-e-Islami (JeI), the PFI, as well as Jihadi organisations.

Urban Naxalism: Theory and Practice

Researches in security studies have focused on understanding unconventional, persistent and unending conflicts in the world by defining and researching generations of warfare. Urban Naxalism falls within the ambit of Fourth Generation Warfare (4GW). In recent years, military thinkers have focused on

4GW, that is, conflicts over ideas and involving at least one non-state actor.

The nature of 4GW is such that it derives legitimacy from genuine developmental issues on the ground. The latest government statistics show that 90 districts in India are currently Naxal affected.[1] All these districts fall within rural areas with extreme levels of poverty and total lack of development. However, the reach of Naxalism is not just limited to rural areas. Their presence in urban areas is part of a Maoist strategy that has been extensively detailed and documented by the central committee of the CPI (M).

The document, 'Strategy and Tactics of the Indian Revolution' (STIR) was issued by the CPI (M) in 2004. In 2003–2004, the former Peoples' War Group (PWG) and the Maoist Communist Centre (MCC), both of which were armed Naxal groups, held a series of discussions to work out a merger. The central committees of both organisations met to discuss and draw out a strategy document for seizing power in India. This document was finalised in September 2004 and coincided with the merger of the PWG and MCC.

The ultimate aim of the Naxals is to achieve an Indian (Communist) revolution. The document in question details the plan for this revolution. The sections of the document that focus on Naxal activities in urban areas provide the theoretical framework of urban Naxalism in India. The term Urban Naxal is thus not an empty term, rather it has a basis in the literature publicly provided by organisations involved in the Naxal movement in India.

The urban movement is one of the main sources, which provides cadres and leadership having various types of capabilities essential for the people's war and for the establishment of liberated area. Moreover, the responsibility for the provision of supplies, technology-expertise, information and other such things, to the people's war, too lies on the shoulders of the urban revolutionary movement itself. Hence Party has to pay special attention to allocate leadership cadres accordingly to work in urban movement.[2]

The above excerpt from the 'Strategy and Tactics' document created by the CPI (Maoist) party clearly details the need for recruits to the 'Urban Naxal cause'. And this has not remained just words. The year 2015–2016 kept India occupied with shocking revelations on the campuses of renowned education institutes like the Film and Television Institute of India (FTII), Hyderabad Central University, Indian Institute of Technology (IIT) Madras, JNU, Osmania University, Jadavpur University and DU. JNU reverberated with slogans that championed the breaking of the Indian nation. All this happened under the cover of constitutional values. In fact, STIR, on page 69–70, mentions the following:

We should not belittle the importance of the fact that the urban areas are the strong centres of the enemy. With this long term perspective, we should develop a secret party, a united front and people's armed elements; intensify the class struggle in the urban areas and mobilise the support of millions of urban masses for the people's war.[3]

One of the strategies outlined in an allied document called the 'Urban Perspective'[4] is to look into possible methods of exploiting ghettos—'a slum or locality inhabited mostly or completely by one community'—by dividing the communities on various emotive issues and by triggering violence/riots. The aim, therefore, is to make firm entries into the ghettos to organise communities to carry forward the movement, among others. This is chillingly similar to the work carried out by Urban Naxals in Muslim-majority areas before the riots happened in North East Delhi.

The Maoist document also focuses on taking advantage of the religious divide between Hindus and Muslims, by proclaiming the latter to be oppressed by 'fascist' Hindus. This is an alarming proposition as it tends to try and inflame a decades-old perceived simmering feud between the two communities, which is not true and must be guarded against at all levels through proactive measures by the government machinery.

The document thus points to a long-term approach of the Maoists towards the urban areas. This would include solidifying their existing bases in urban areas, trying to penetrate the industrial working class, trade unions, unorganised labour, white-collar employees, youth bodies and NGOs. Under the current circumstances, they are required to provide logistical support to the Maoists operating in rural areas by way of supplying arms, ammunition, medicines, food supplies, footwear, clothing, spare parts, communication equipment, batteries, etc. Additionally, they could provide further impetus to mobilise what are considered to be front organisations— media, social activists and human right activists—to espouse their cause. They have also analysed the use of cyber warfare,[5] which is intended to be used more in the urban environment due to higher penetration of the internet in such areas. Though not given out in detail, they probably intend to progressively target vital installations, crucial networks like financial networks, security networks and essential services, which today run on the internet, and social networks to profess their ideology and spread their propaganda. Dr S. Radhakrishnan, in the University Education Commission Report, clearly delineated the function of universities:

Universities are the intellectual sanctuaries of the inner life of the nation. They must train intellectual pioneers, seeking guidance from the past but providing dynamics to realise new dreams.[6]

From the year 2015 onwards, the country watched aghast as these sanctuaries of education turned into theatres of secession.

This, however, was just an implosion. The groundwork for Urban Naxalism has been created meticulously in our universities for decades. As per newspaper reports, in 2014, G.N. Saibaba, a professor of English at DU, was arrested by the Maharashtra police for links with Maoists. In 2017, a session's court in Maharashtra's Gadchiroli district convicted him to life imprisonment. Four others, including former JNU student Hem Mishra and former journalist Prashant Rahi, were also convicted along with the DU professor and sentenced to imprisonment for life. In 2016, newspaper reports also carried headlines of tribals from Sukma filing a first information report (FIR) for murder against prominent intellectuals from DU and other institutions, alleging that they had a hand in the murder of Shamnath Baghel, a prominent anti-Naxal activist. Professors of Delhi universities and other urban intellectuals and CPI [Marxist] office bearers were named in the FIR filed by Baghel's wife.[7,8] Though the ultimate outcome of the case was relief by the Supreme Court, dismissal due to lack of evidence,[9] clean chit by the Chattisgarh Police, and compensation by the NHRC, the case is an interesting area of research into the politics and strategies of Urban Naxalism and the terrible predicament the tribals of the Naxal belt face due to Naxal violence and its urban support.

The following excerpt from the STIR document clearly shows the spine-chilling outlook for students, teachers and security forces in the country.

We have to also pay special attention to our work among women, students, youth, teachers and middle-class intellectuals.... Youth and cultural organisations also play a good role in the activities of the city movement ... it is our task to further deepen our activities within the student community. Considering the present situation we should develop suitable organisational forms to imbue them with revolutionary politics, and organise and mobilise the vast majority of them politically. They can be mobilised politically on both domestic and international issues.

It is very important to penetrate into the military, para-military forces, police, and higher levels of the administrative machinery of the state. It is necessary to obtain information regarding the enemy, to build support for the revolution within these organs, and even to incite revolt when the time is ripe.... However for certain crucial things there is need for support from the urban areas. Depending on its strength, the urban organisation should make all efforts to provide such support. Supplies or contacts for supplies of certain types of materials such as arms and ammunition, spare parts, medical supplies, etc., are only available in the urban areas. Technical help in the form of repairs and maintenance of fighting, communication and other equipment of the PLGA, development of new technologies for the people's war, and sending comrades with technical, electrical, electronic and other skills to settle in the countryside is another task of the urban organisation. Propaganda and publications to fulfil the needs of the rural movement is also one of the important tasks in the urban centres.[10]

It is evident that multi-directional attacks are being planned by Urban Naxals to uproot democracy. Urban Naxalism is a unique threat to India. This problem cannot be tackled by the government alone. The need is to create awareness amongst citizens and especially the urban youth about the phenomenon of Urban Naxalism that views them as potential recruits and as cannon fodder for a Maoist revolution.

Jihadism: Theory and Organisations

The core philosophy of Jihadism in India has an explicit connection with the idea of Khilafat, which was historically a movement of Muslims around the end of First World War, and later re-emerged as the ISIS in Syria and Iraq in 2014. The idea behind both the movements is the restoration of the Khilafat or the rule of the Islamic Khalifa. Many contemporary movements like the JeI, which are influenced by the ideas of Abdul A'la Madudi, Islamic scholar and founder of the JeI, also form the core of the Islamist ideology in India.

The Ideas of Jihad

Two sources tell us the details of the ideology of jihad. Historically, it is revealing to study the ideas of the khilafat and the corresponding ideas of leaders of the Khilafat Movement in Kerala, such as Ali Muslaiyar. The ideas of these leaders have great traction amongst the Islamic youth who were at the forefront in Shaheen Bagh and other movements that led to the

Delhi riots. The other is a contemporary study of the ideas of ISIS and Ghazwa-e-Hind.

The Khilafat Movement started in India with the dissolution of the Ottoman Empire in 1919 after the end of the First World War. This was seen as an affront by Muslims all over the world. Muslims in India rallied for a restoration of the Khalifa. The movement launched by them, which had received Mahatma Gandhi's support, had unfortunately led to the violent annihilation of Hindus in communal violence like the Moplah riots. The violence was an extended version of the movement in Kerala in 1921. The then government had declared the Congress and Khilafat meetings illegal. So, a reaction in Kerala began against the crackdown by the British in Ernad and Valluvanad taluks of Malabar.

Khilafat meetings in the Malabar borrowed so much from Islamist terminology and ideology that the movement firmly turned against the Hindu landlords of the region. It became a riot of the kudiyans or Moplahs against the Hindu *jenmis* or landlords.[11] The leaders of this rebellion were Variyankunnath Kunjahammed Haji, Sithi Koya Thangal of Kumaranpathor and Ali Muslaiyar. Some of these leaders have now emerged as idols of the anti-CAA protesters in Jamia Millia Islamia (JMI) and Shaheen Bagh, etc.

Historically, the formation of the JeI in 1941 and the crystallisation of an extreme Islamic ideology under Abdul A'la Madudi gave a fillip to the ideology of jihad.

Jihad fi Sabilillah is explained in Madudi's works: 'to alter peoples' outlook and spark a mental and intellectual revolution through the medium of speech and the written word is a form of jihad. To change the old tyrannical system and establish a just order by the power of the sword is also jihad.'[12]

By default, this 'just order' is Islam. Madudi clearly lays down the contours for an Islamic takeover of not just India but the world. Islam is defined 'not as a religion' but as a revolutionary ideology. Nations are not recognised. The ultimate end is the establishment of Islam on Earth.

These ideas are seen in the ISIS movement in contemporary times. In its first issue, *Dabiq*, the organisation's online magazine, explained the ISIS stand on *tawhid* (monotheism), *manhaj* (methodology), *hijrah* (migration), jihad (holy Islamic war), and *jama'ah* (Islamic congregation).

The ISIS worldview is as follows:

O Ummah of Islam, indeed the world today has been divided into two camps and two trenches, with no third camp present: The camp of Islam and faith, and the camp of kufr (disbelief) and hypocrisy – the camp of the Muslims and the mujahidin everywhere, and the camp of the Jews, the crusaders, their allies, and with them the rest of the nations and religions of kufr, all being led by America and Russia, and being mobilised by the Jews.[11]

In a revealing parallel with the ideology of the JeI, one of the prime goals of ISIS is the creation of a Sunni Islamic State. The recent attempt at establishing a Khilafat was led by Caliph Abu Bakr al-Baghdadi, who claims his ancestry from Prophet Mohammed. In the same frame as the legendary Rashidun Khalifas, he demanded the allegiance of all Muslims across the world. Like the JeI, the ISIS also believes that all religions which agree to democracy have to die because human laws have no place as Allah has already done that through his messenger in the form of the Sharia.

This global Khilafat movement has joined hands with many such movements in India, the JeI being only one such ideological movement. According to a number of reports of the Soufan Center, a non-profit organisation funded by the United Nations Democracy Fund, in November 2015, 23 Indian nationals were fighting for the ISIS in Iraq and Syria.[12] There is only one known case of an Indian returning, that of Arif Majeed, who left for Syria with three other friends from the western Indian state of Maharashtra. While nothing has since been heard about these three, Arif returned to India in

November 2015 with help from the Indian government and has been undergoing interrogation.

The ISIS released a 22-minute video[13] in April 2016 in Arabic featuring three young Indian-born men allegedly speaking from an ISIS-controlled area. They acknowledged that they are in Sham and gave an insight into their plans.

They stated that they were really happy and satisfied in a land run strictly according to the Sharia and that they hated India, the land where people worshiped animals and trees. They vowed to return, but only to invade. They proclaimed that they would come on horseback with swords in their hands to slaughter the kafirs (non-believers).

Incidentally, Kerala has been one of the main states for conversion and subsequent recruitment of women into the ISIS. In July 2016, it came to light that at least 11 persons from the state, including women and children, were in ISIS-controlled territory.[14]

More recently, a news video report titled *Khorasan Files: The Journey of Indian 'Islamic State' Widows*[15] depicted the account of women from Kerala who were a part of the ISIS. Converts from Christianity, they found their way to Syria with their husbands. The death of their spouses left them widowed with children to raise. The conversion of Christian and Hindu girls to Islam in Kerala and their subsequent radicalisation into ISIS ideology has promoted allegations of 'Love Jihad' from Christian and Hindu organisations as well as the Kerala High Court. In 2009, while hearing a bail application of two persons involved in the conversion of non-Muslim girls to Islam, Justice K.T. Sankaran had observed that there was a concerted effort at conversion by some outfits in Kerala.

A number of organisations in India are allied to the core jihadi ideology of the Khilafat and the ISIS. Some of them are the Students Islamic Movement of India (SIMI), the youth wing of the JeI, which was subsequently banned. The Indian Mujahideen (IM), in turn, was a mutated version of SIMI which itself is the largest Islamic radical mobilisation India has seen.

The core ideology of SIMI was similar to its parent organisation.[16] Its core aim is the establishment of an Islamic state in India. Ideological viewpoints include governing human life on the basis of the Quran, and the propagation of Islam and jihad for the cause of Islam. The SIMI rejects secularism, democracy, western ideals and nationalism as ideas against the will of Allah. Its focus is on the restoration of the Khilafat (caliphate), emphasis on the ummah (Muslim brotherhood) and the need for a jihad to establish the supremacy of Islam.

SIMI was formed at Aligarh in UP on 25 April 1977. Mohammad Ahmadullah Siddiqi, a professor of journalism and public relations at the Western Illinois University, Macomb, in the US state of Illinois, was its founding president.

After the demolition of the Babri Masjid in 1992, SIMI undertook radical and aggressive posturing. A blanket ban was imposed on the organisation in 2001 under the Prevention of Terrorism Act (POTA). The ban was lifted in 2008 only to be re-imposed again in 2008.

The ban, however, did not lead to its end. Its cadres only regrouped under a new name and that was how the Indian Mujahideen (IM) came into being in 2008, carrying out a spate of terror attacks across India. During this period, parallel jihadist groups led by figures who knew the IM leadership from their time in SIMI proliferated as well.

The central point is that the jihadist networks in India remain extremely fluid and consist of small groups of individuals who are loosely allied together. Another jihadist organisation that has connections to the riots in the capital is the Popular Front of India. This organisation was established in 2006 as a federation of the Karnataka Forum for Dignity (KFD), the National Development Front (NDF), Kerala and the Manitha Neethi Pasarai (MNP), Tamil Nadu. It describes itself as a 'socio-economic movement' which aims to empower Muslims as well as the deprived and the downtrodden in the nation at large.[17] Law enforcement agencies in Kerala have even found evidence of the use of lethal weapons in PFI centres. The outfit also has a political arm, called the Social Democratic Party of India (SDPI).

SDPI was established in 2009 and was registered with the Election Commission of India in 2010. The website describes the party as follows:

founded for the advancement and uniform development of all the citizenry including Muslims, Dalits, Backward Classes and Adivasis.... The party is here to fight the neo-colonial and neo-liberal incursions in our country.

The Urban Naxal–Jihadi Link and the Delhi Riots

The Urban Naxal–Jihadi link in the Delhi riots can be seen in the leaders and cadre of the aforementioned outfits who were actively present at anti-CAA protest sites. Most of these protest

Social media posts of both girls went viral after the Jamia Millia Islamia violence.

Ladeeda Sakhaloon
April 23 at 12:49 AM · Facebook for Android · 🌐

Hehehehe

Ladeeda Sakhaloon April 22, 2017 at 11:35 AM · Facebook for Android · 🌐

Dont understimate the power of HIJABI . 😎

Ladeeda Sakhaloon
14 Dec at 11:30 AM · 🌐

Chekh Oov Writes
During the protest gathering happened
yesterday. Some liberals dictated us to refrain
from chanting " Insha Allah " and " Allahu Akbar
" . We have only submitted completely towards
Almighty. We have abandoned your secular
slogans long before . Those slogans will be
raised loudly again and again. Those slogans
are our spirit , our imagination and the one
which refines our existence. You might be in a
hurry to prove your secular loyalty , but we are
not. We are and will exist in every space as

sites in North East Delhi subsequently imploded into large-scale communal violence after a period of rapidly escalating street violence.

Most of the images and data used in this section are from social media profiles of individuals belonging to these groups.[18] One of the most enduring images of the campus violence in Delhi's JMI on 15 December 2019 was of the media-promoted 'Sheroes'. These were Ladeeda Sakhaloon and Ayesha Renna N, both students of the university.

However, further research revealed that both girls are intricately related to the jihadi network in Kerala. Ayesha's husband is a news contributor (journalist), of a news portal called India Tomorrow English, while Ladeeda's husband, Shiyas, is the secretary of the Kerala-headquartered Student's Islamic Organisation (SIO), which also has support from the Peoples' Democratic Party (PDP) of Kerala.

Ladeeda and her husband with Abdul Nazher Mahdani, the president of the PDP.

The SIO was propped as the student wing of JeI Hind after the government banned SIMI because of their terror activities in India. S.Q.R. Ilyas, the father of controversial JNU student, Umar Khalid was associated with SIMI. He is currently the president of the Welfare Party of India.

Interestingly, both the girls are associated with the same party and are supporters of the Kerala-based PDP too.

Who is Mahdani? Probably the most powerful person in Kerala, he has been accused of two major terror attacks in India. First, on 14 February 1998, serial bomb explosions rocked the venue of the Bharatiya Janata Party's (BJP's) election rally in Coimbatore, Tamil Nadu, in which 58 people were dead and almost 200 injured. L.K. Advani, who was meant to address the rally, narrowly missed the attack as he did not reach there on time. The Tamil Nadu police arrested Mahdani. On 15 March 2006, however, on the day of Holi, a very urgent and special assembly session was called up by Congress-led United Democratic Front (UDF) government in Kerala. The opposition at the time was the CPI (M)-led Left Democratic Front (LDF). The house unanimously passed the resolution to free him on humanitarian grounds. He got bail in 2007. And all three political parties gave him a heroic welcome. Exactly one year after his release, on 25 July 2008, Bengaluru witnessed nine serial blasts. SIMI was the main conspirator of this attack, along with Mahdani. Currently, he is under trial and is in Bengaluru.

A number of students have been arrested or charge-sheeted in connection with the Delhi riots, including Sharjeel Imam, Safoora Zargar, Devangna Kalita and Natasha Narwal. Recently, 35-year-old Meeran Haider, a member of the youth wing of Rashtriya Janta Dal (RJD) and student of JMI has been arrested for planning the riots.

The Urban Naxal connection is seen from the activation of networks in JNU, JMI and DU during the months leading to the riots. This included the activation of cultural organisations to sustain and mobilise the Shaheen Bagh and other anti-CAA protest sites in Delhi. It can be seen in the media interest generated in the protest sites. Ideas of jihad also took a centre stage in the many speeches that were made, including the much-publicised speech by Sharjeel Imam.

Conclusion

The Delhi riots clearly mirror Urban–Naxal Jihadi theories of revolution and jihad as exemplified and detailed in the literature emerging from these organisations. Much research is needed on the networks that operated from front organisations in public universities and institutions of repute in Delhi. Much of the empirical data about the role of such organisations in the riots is also in the public domain in the form of videos, photographs and speeches of the ultra-Left and jihadi cadre present in North East Delhi in the months preceding the riots. More research would be needed to analyse this data and strengthen the thesis in this chapter.

References

1. Data on Maoist-affected districts was revised by the central government in 2018. Earlier, this figure stood at 182 districts in 2011 as per data on the South Asian Terrorism Portal.

2. For a general outline of the 'Strategy and Tactics Document', see https://www.vifindia.org/MAOIST-STRATEGY-DOCUMENT-ANALYSIS. Available on https://www. satp.org/satporgtp/countries/india/maoist/documents/papers/ strategy.htm.

3. Ibid.

4. For details on the Urban Perspective, see https://www. satp. org/satporgtp/countries/india/maoist/documents/papers/ Urbanperspective.htm.

5. For details about how social media is harnessed in modern warfare, see Knopf, Christina and Eric Ziegelmeyer. 2012. 'Fourth Generation Warfare and the US Military's Social Media Strategy', *ASPJ Africa and Francophonie*, Vol. 3(24). Available at https://www.airuniversity.af.edu/Portals/10/ASPJ_French/ journals_E/ Volume-03_Issue-4/2012_4_e.pdf.

6. Radhakrishnan, S. 1949. 'University Education Commission 1948–49', University Education Commission Report. Available at https://www.educationforallinindia.com/1949%20Report%20 of%20the%20University%20Education%.pdf.

7. Mishra, Ritesh. 2016. Nandini Sundar used fake name in Chhattisgarh, faces strict action: Top cop, https://www. hindustantimes.com/india-news/bastar-police-for-strict-action-against-nandini-sundar-du-professor-booked-for-tribal-s-murder/ story-zeGWeFdQUjdBlOWTxz3a8J.html, downloaded on 20 April 2020

8. PTI. 2016. Chhattisgarh: Case against DU professor Nandini Sundar over tribal man's murder, https://www.deccanchronicle. com/nation/crime/081116/chhattisgarh-case-against-du-professor -nandini-sundar-over-tribal-mans-murder.html

9. FP Staff. 2019. DU professor Nandini Sundar, five others cleared of all charges in 2016 Sukma murder case as cops find no proof against them, https://www.firstpost.com/india/du-professor-nandini-sundar-five-others-cleared-of-all-charges-in-2016-sukma-murder-case-chhattisgarh-police-find-no-evidence-against-them-6068841.html, downloaded on April 20, 2020.

10. For the 'Strategy and Tactics Document', see https://www.vifindia.org/MAOIST-STRATEGY-DOCUMENT-ANALYSIS. The entire document is available at https://www.satp.org/satporgtp/countries/india/maoist/documents/papers/strategy. htm.

11. For details of the Moplah rebellion, see https://www.gktoday.in/gk/moplah-rebellion-1921/ accessed on 2 April 2020.

12. For the Jamaat-e-Islami's position on jihad, see https://www.muslim-library.com/dl/books/English_Jihad_in_ Islam.pdf.

13. *Dabiq*, Vol. 1, p. 4, corresponding author may be contacted for a copy.

14. Three important reports pertaining to foreign fighters can be found at https://thesoufancenter.org/research/.

15. For the news byte in reference to the 22-minute Arabic video, see https://www.youtube.com/watch?v=g7rlFOvhHRY.

16. Surendran, Vivek. 2016. 'ISIS Recruits from Kerala: 11 Out of 22 Missing Keralites Suspected to Be in Syria', *India Today*, 11 July. Available at indiatoday.intoday.in/story/isis-kerala-recruitment-syria-kasargod-pinarayivijayan/1/712168.html.

17. For *India's Most Wanted in the Islamic State: The Khorasan Confessions*, see https://www.youtube.com/watch?v=9s1h RVFR0t0.

18. For information about SIMI, see https://www.satp.org/satporgtp/countries/india/terroristoutfits/ simi.htm.

19. For information about the PFI, see http://www.popularfrontindia.org/.

20. We are aware that social media posts used in this chapter are private opinion. We have simply used them to build a larger picture.

THREE

THE BACKGROUND TO THE DELHI RIOTS 2020: THE CITIZENSHIP AMENDMENT ACT (CAA)

You must make a difference between Hindu refugees and Muslim immigrants and the country must take responsibility of the refugees.

– Prime Minister Jawaharlal Nehru's letter to the then chief minister of Assam, Gopinath Bordoloi, May 1949

I refuse the fact that we should not care about the Hindus of Pakistan since they are Pakistani citizens. Irrespective of citizenship of Pakistan's Hindus, it is our duty to protect them like we protect Indian Muslims and Hindus.

– Dr Ram Manohar Lohia (translated) as quoted by PM Narendra Modi in his speech in parliament, 6 February 2020

Introduction

The Citizenship Amendment Act (CAA) 2019, around which the initial anti-government movement was formed in December 2019 was tabled in the Indian parliament on 9 December 2019. It was passed by the Lok Sabha on 10 December 2019, with 311 members of parliament (MPs) voting in favour and 80 against the bill. It was passed by the

Rajya Sabha on 11 December 2019, with 125 votes in favour and 105 votes against. The law became effective from 10 January 2020. A reading of the law shows that it is a timed intervention targeted at minorities suffering religious persecution in three of India's neighbouring, Muslim-majority countries—Pakistan, Afghanistan and Bangladesh. Under this amendment, migrants who had entered India before 31 December 2014 and had suffered or feared religious persecution in their country of origin were eligible for citizenship. The amendment also relaxed the residence requirement for the naturalisation of these migrants from eleven to five years.

According to IB records, 31,313 people (25,447 Hindus, 5,807 Sikhs, 55 Christians, 2 Buddhists and 2 Parsis) will be immediate beneficiaries of the Act. There is nothing in the law that stops the government from framing laws for religious groups belonging to other neighbouring countries, which could be considered to be left out of this amendment to the citizenship Act, as is being alleged. There are yet a number of communities, for instance, the Sri Lankan Tamils who need proactive policy legislation as regards citizenship. The government should and most likely will consider such communities for the provision of relief.[1]

The Act does not apply to Indian citizens. The fact that it has been made a pivot of protests led by the Urban Naxal–Jihadi circuit all over India merits deeper analysis.

The protests need to be seen in the background of the National Democratic Alliance (NDA) being elected to the centre with an overwhelming majority in two successive elections, in 2014 and in 2019. Both mandates have been under the leadership of Narendra Modi. A number of key policy changes were successfully tabled and seen through in NDA's second term (NDA 2.0). Of these, doing away of Article 370 of the Indian Constitution and the resolution of the Ram Janmabhoomi dispute are significant steps. They will be discussed here as a background to the anti-government protests engineered under the guise of anti-CAA protests, which ultimately culminated in the 2020 riots in Delhi.

The reading down of Articles 370 and 35-A of the Indian Constitution were strong steps taken by the current government. Complex geopolitical factors that had given birth to and sustained the narrative of Kashmir being a disputed territory became neutralised. Jammu and Kashmir, and Ladakh too, were declared as union territories. The region finally saw the dawn of governance based on equal rights for all citizens. However, under the Urban Naxal–Jihadi combine, this was framed as an anti-Muslim decision.

The second significant move under NDA 2.0 was the resolution of the decades-long Ram Janmabhoomi issue which had been exploited by political parties for decades to deepen the wedge between Hindus and Muslims. This, too, was resolved peacefully, sending a clear message that in India, syncretism symbolised by structures like the Cheraman Juma Masjid in Kerala can be a part of the Indian identity but not assaultive structures like the Babri Masjid.[2]

The Historical Background to CAA

The partition of India along religious lines was the first time in the known, recorded history of the nation when a territory and people were rent asunder due to religious identity. The idea that there are 'two nations' on this land; one the Islamic and the other non-Islamic is an alien idea that dominated the circumstances leading up to the Partition.[3] The same was eerily similar to what the country witnessed around the anti-CAA agitations. It was the same India which had been under continuous Muslim rule over large parts of the land since the since 12th century. While Partition was accepted by the contemporary political dispensation, the transfer of populations was not acceptable as a principle governing the two-nation theory. The resultant transfer of populations was a tragic, unacceptable consequence of succumbing to Islamic identity politics. Even today, there are pools of Hindu population in Pakistan. The Tharparkar area of Sindh is a Hindu-majority area. Chittagong, which was part of erstwhile East Pakistan (now Bangladesh), was a Buddhist-majority area with 13 Chittagong hill tract tribes living in the region, not even one of which were Islamic.[4]

The fate of minorities in Pakistan and Bangladesh is a question that has been around since 1947. The weak assurances and the absence of guarantees in the Nehru–Liaquat Pact, signed on 8 April 1950, condemned Hindus, Sikhs and Christians in Pakistan and later Bangladesh to utter decimation. This is revealed by population growth figures of both countries. Similar situations were faced by Hindus and Sikhs in Afghanistan. The CAA seeks to address the plight and rights of these communities in Pakistan, Bangladesh and Afghanistan. The Act seems to recognise India as a natural home for these populations.

Narratives around the CAA

The CAA has dominated public discourse in India since December 2019. However, a large part of the discourse has been against the Act, which has been, for the most part, for the wrong reasons. People have been out on the streets showing their resistance and protesting throughout the country. Protests are perfectly acceptable in a democracy if there is a genuine reason for them, are harmless and within the constitutional limits. However, that is not the case with the anti-CAA protests, as they have neither been based on genuine reasons nor have they been harmless. Fostering militaristic aggression to fill the minds of a section of the society with hatred can lead to no positive outcome.

The Shaheen Bagh protest site was created by blocking one major road in South East Delhi for more than three months.

In a sprawling metropolitan city, commuting is an important aspect of daily life, as large numbers of people go about their work. The occupation of non-designated public spaces such as main roads by the protestors at Shaheen Bagh, as well as at other sites, has caused inconvenience to thousands of commuters every day.

Since the anti-CAA protests began nationwide, public and private property worth crores of rupees was vandalised in violent street protests. The biggest loss of human lives occurred in Delhi on 23–25 February 2020 as the anti-CAA protests took an ugly turn. Approximately 53 persons are reported to have died and a huge loss of property has occurred during these three days.[5]

Propaganda to Create Unrest

The anti-CAA protesters did not have verifiable and sustainable facts and arguments in their favour. A pack of lies had been spread around and a heavy dose of fear-mongering was inflicted on a majority of Muslims in the country. The reasons for the protest kept changing since day one of the protest marches and establishment of sites such as Shaheen Bagh.

First, they argued that an anti-Muslim Act had been passed. However, the fact is that the word 'Muslim' has not even once been used in the amended Act. The Act has made an additional special provision for expediting cases of citizenship in cases of six religious minorities of the three neighbouring Islamic countries, Pakistan, Bangladesh and Afghanistan who have faced religious persecution and have entered India till 31 December 2014.

The Act is to grant citizenship, not to take it away from anyone, including Muslims. Most of the protesters were made to believe that populations of Hindus, Sikhs, Jains, Buddhists, Parsis and Christians from these countries were to be allowed to enter the country anytime, whereas Muslims would not be entertained.

Moreover, fear was being perpetuated that Indian Muslims would be thrown out on some pretext. Unfortunately, this propaganda was used by none other than the chief minister of Delhi, Arvind Kejriwal. He had commented: 'Where the people will go. Their forefathers were born here....' Contrary to such fear-mongering, however, statistics prove that in the last six years, hundreds of Muslims have been granted citizenship out of the total 4,000 cases from Pakistan, Afghanistan and Bangladesh.[6] Further, as the CAA does not apply to any citizen of India, there is no question of anyone's citizenship being taken away and hence, the protestors' fears are ill-founded.

One argument has been that the Act is discriminatory and is a violation of the fundamental right to equality provided through Article 14 of the Constitution of India. However, it has also been settled that the CAA does not apply to Indian citizens. It does not stand to reason that CAA 2019 violates the right to equality ensured to Indian citizens.

Another contest against the CAA has been that it is a violation of the Assam Accord of 1985. The concerns of Assam and other north-eastern states with respect to the CAA are very different from the propaganda being created in other parts of the country. Briefly, Assam does not want any outsiders in the State whether Hindu or Muslim. Further, the CAA does not pose any threat to preserving the social, cultural and linguistic identity of places (mainly in the Northeast) covered under the Sixth Schedule of the Constitution. The issues that the people in Assam have against the CAA are entirely different and cannot be conflated with the protests in Delhi and elsewhere in the country.

Non-BJP governments in Kerala, Punjab, Rajasthan, Madhya Pradesh (MP), Chhattisgarh and West Bengal have added to the controversy by declaring that they will not implement the amended law in their respective states.[7] They have done so despite the well-known fact that the issue of citizenship does not fall within the purview of states.

Citizenship is a subject of the central list of the Seventh Schedule of the Constitution and hence the statement by the states is simply political posturing.

Most of the arguments given in opposing the CAA prove to be misguided when seen in light of facts. When the opponents of the Act could not give any solid reason to back their arguments, they started fuelling further controversy over imaginary ogres. They created a fresh contestation that CAA is fine but it would be discriminatory for Muslims once combined with the National Register of Citizens (NRC) and the National Population Register (NPR).[8]

Till date the NRC has been conducted only in Assam; that, too, was a requirement due to the Assam Accord and was implemented by the Supreme Court. Rules are yet to be drafted for a pan-India NRC. Its roadmap is not yet ready to be implemented throughout India and it will be subject to constitutional limits and scrutiny whenever it is prepared. Moreover, it needs to be passed by both the houses of parliament, like any other legislation.

The NPR is not something new. The 2004 amendment in the Citizenship Act 1955 made it compulsory to register every citizen of India and the responsibility was entrusted to the union government. The first NPR exercise was done in 2010 and was updated in 2015. The idea was to have a comprehensive database of Indian citizens so that government schemes, programmes and benefits reach the target citizens. It is meant to help in better planning and implementation and is not related to CAA.

A big confusion has been intentionally created to fan unrest and social polarisation. Broadly speaking, the common Muslim has been made to believe that the present regime at the centre will ask for their documents and in case they fail to furnish the required documents, they will be deported or put in detention centres. Although they seem to be clueless on where they will be deported and where such detention centres are being created which can accommodate the huge population of the country (around 15 per cent), which has been fed this canard.

Content created in fake news factories and widely shared on social media has added fuel to the already lit fire of Islamic fundamentalism. During the earliest protest at JMI, fake news about deaths of some Jamia students at the hands of the Delhi police was spread by a few Muslim journalists from Kerala. Then, unfortunately, another fake video was shared by AAP leader and deputy chief minister of Delhi, Manish Sisodia, that the Delhi police had torched buses near Jamia Nagar during the anti-CAA protests. But it was later proved that no such incident of bus burning by any policeman of the Delhi police happened.[9] This started a barrage of fake material shared on social media to create disturbance in society.

The fact remains that the CAA has been passed in both houses of parliament and accorded approval by the president of India on 12 December 2019 as it became a law. Post the Delhi riots, Indian National Congress (INC) leader Kapil Sibal had to admit in the parliament that contrary to his previous stand, the Act does not apply to any Muslim of the country. If anyone still has any doubt against its validity, he or she can, of course, take a legal course of action. The CAA has already been challenged in the Supreme Court through several petitions. After hearing a batch of 143 writ petitions, however, the honourable court has not 'stayed' the implementation of the CAA.[10]

Bare Facts about the CAA

By granting some relaxation to six minorities from three neighbouring countries through CAA, the union government has not violated any precedent. It has a right to grant citizenship under the Indian Citizenship Act to any special category of citizenship seekers. The union governments in the past have been exercising their right, whether it was related to Tamils of Indian origin in Sri Lanka or Burmese people of Indian origin.[11]

The union home minister Amit Shah presented the rationale of the Act in detail in both the houses of parliament during discussions on the bill. He spoke with facts on how the minorities in the three countries have been facing religious persecution over the years.[12] The partition of this country had taken place on the basis of religion and it is the civilisational and constitutional obligation of our country to give relief to the minorities of these three states and alleviate their misery. To put forth his arguments, he also quoted eminent leaders of the country from yesteryears, including the makers of the Constitution of India.

Further, the Citizenship Amendment Bill (CAB) was not new; it had been in the public domain since 2016 and was cleared by a 30-member committee of parliamentarians.[13] The union government had brought almost the same bill in both houses of parliament on 10 and 11 December 2019. After becoming a law, it came to be known as the Citizenship Amendment Act, 2019. Nevertheless, it has invited a barrage of opposing statements and comments after it became a law. Since then, it has been in discourse in the mainstream and social media among other avenues.

Muslim Radicalisation and the Role of the Left in the Anti-CAA Protests and Violence

As the CAA became a law on 12 December 2019 after the approval of the president, voices against it started coming from many corners. Beginning 15 December 2019, anti-CAA protests began across campuses in the capital, from JMI to JNU and others. Before long, the protests appeared pan-India. Muslims were brought at the forefront as they were made to believe that it was a fight for their survival. The Left fuelled this feeling with the support of opposition parties and Islamic fundamental organisations. The imprint of the Left has been clearly visible from the way the anti-CAA protests have been held.

Historically, the Left in the country has always used Islamic fundamentalism as its striking arm. In the 1940s, the Communists had made some cadres join Muslim League who essentially fuelled the two-nation theory and led effectively to Partition. Later in independent India, it strategically worked in 'coordination' with the Congress, particularly during Indira Gandhi's regime. The Left, with its doctrine of India as a State with multiple nations, has always shed tears for minorities, but has often sided with fundamentalist Islamic positions, such as opposition to legislation against the patriarchal triple talaq, rather than with progressive Muslims.[14]

Coming back to the anti-CAA protests, it has become clear that they have been coordinated by Muslim fundamentalists and ultra-Left organisations. Muslim women leading from the front have been a part of the strategy. Terms such as dadi and nani, given to the old women sitting at the iconic Shaheen Bagh dharna, are a part of the tactics to further their propaganda.

Art has also been used as a tool to radicalise people during the anti-CAA protests. This is a typical Leftist way of conducting protests. Poems, songs, graffiti and slogans have been abundantly used day and night at the 24-hour protest sites and marches. Islamic religious calls and Hindu phobic slogans have been spoken under the garb of opposing CAA, such as 'Tera mera rishta kya, la ilaha ill allah' (Our relationship is that there is no God but Allah—from the Islamic creed), 'Allah hu Akbar' (Allah is Great), 'Hindutva ki kabar khudegi, Hinduon se azadi (The grave for Hindutva will be dug. Freedom from Hindus), etc. Hindu religious symbols too have been insulted during anti-CAA protests.

Secessionist slogans have been amply used, like 'Bharat Mata se azadi' (Freedom from India), 'Kashmir ki azadi' (Freedom for Kashmir), 'Jinnah wali azadi' (The Jinnah type of freedom), etc. The Free Kashmir placard was held by protesters in Mumbai. Eyewitnesses told us that Pakistan

Zindabad was shouted at an anti-CAA protest programme. Faiz Ahmed Faiz's poem, 'Hum Dekhenge' too has been used to fuel controversy. Small children are being radicalised and their minds being poisoned. Hundreds of hate speeches at anti-CAA protests have added to the hatred building up during these months.

Meanwhile, the ecosystem of radical Leftists in media and academia has tried to build a fake narrative in the international media that the CAA is an anti-Muslim law and the present union government is anti-Muslim. However, it has become evident now that the CAA is just an opportunity to vent piled-up angst against the huge victory of the NDA government in May 2019 and the bold steps taken by it afterwards, the most important being setting aside Articles 370 and 35-A and making the oppressive instant triple talaq illegal. The Supreme Court judgment on the long-pending Ayodhya issue in favour of Ram Janmabhoomi has created additional anti-government issues.

Conclusion

Though the protesters tried to make anti-CAA protests an all-religion activity, eventually most of them remained Muslim protests with extreme religious sloganeering. From a secular-looking movement, it became an exclusively Muslim movement. Non-Muslims were embarrassed by hard-hitting Islamic slogans. Efforts were aimed at making it look like a secular affair but ultimately, hatred fed through protests led to communal violence and rioting. Anti-CAA, anti-NRC, anti-NPR protests eventually became a protest against all other religions of the country, anti-police, anti-government and anti-India. Questioning the integrity of the country became the norm and police was targeted time and again as a 'tool of state oppression'.

Dissent and protesting is fine. However, under the garb of anti-CAA protests, demeaning Hindu symbols is wrong. Shouting separatist and secessionist slogans against the country clearly fuels fissiparous forces. Vandalising public and private property and attacking the police leads to lawlessness.

Heavy doses of extreme Islamic fundamentalism during these months have poisoned some Muslim minds to the extent that the protests which began with the chanting of the Preamble to the Constitution have culminated in the killings of poor people belonging to scheduled communities. 'Samvidhan bachao, desh bachao' (Save the Constitution, save the country) protests have culminated in the mob lynching of Vinod Kashyap, a scheduled caste person, and the shooting of Dinesh Khatik, another scheduled caste person, by rioters in North East Delhi on 24 February 2020. Sharpshooting from high-rise buildings (reminiscent of happenings in Egypt and Syria) in the neighbourhood and the brutal killing of IB officer Ankit Sharma are the unfortunate fallout of a coordinated strategy to politicise a government policy. The protests which began with photos of Mahatma Gandhi and Dr B.R. Ambedkar and the unfurling of the Tricolour sadly ended with the Tricolour being used in making petrol bombs and torching shops and houses. The 'iconic' Shaheen Bagh Model, eventually culminated in and set the stage for communal violence, a first of its kind in Delhi in contemporary times.

References

1. Angma D. Jhala. 2013. Daughters of the Hills: 'Legacies of Colonialism, Nationalism and Religious Communalism in the Chakma Raj Family, Chittagong Hill Tracts, Bengal c.1900–1972, *South Asian History and Culture*, p. 107.

2. Bagriya, A. 2019. 'Supreme Court Refuses Stay on Citizenship Amendment Act, Issues Notice to Centre', *Hindustan Times*, 18 December. https://www.hindustantimes.com/india-news/supreme-court-refuses-stay-on-citizenship-amendment-act-issues-notice-to-centre/story-hXDK5Qx27bmX9AtLORBVYP.html.

3. Beg, M.A. 2013. Social & Environmental Baseline of Tharparkar District (accessed on 25 April 2020).

4. Chatterji, J. 2010. *The Spoils of Partition*, p. 166. Cambridge: Cambridge University Press.

5. Indo-Asian News Service (IANS). 2019. 'Citizenship Amendment Act 2019: All You Need to Know', *Livemint*, 15 December. Available at https://www.livemint.com/news/india/citizenship-amendment-act-2019-all-you-need-to-know-11576401546515.html.

6. Parthasarathi P.T. 2016. 'Cheraman Perumal between Legend and History: A Search of His Existence in Kerala History', Heritage University of Kerala, 28 November. Available on http://www.heritageuniversityofkerala.com/JournalPDF/Volume4/28.pdf (accessed on 22 April 2020).

7. Press Trust of India (PTI). 2019. '2,830 People from Pakistan, 912 from Afghanistan Given Citizenship in Last 6 Yrs, Many Muslims: Officials', *India Today*, 18 December. Available at https://www.indiatoday.in/india/story/2-830-people-from-pakistan-912-from-afghanistan-given-citizenship-in-last-6-yrs-many-muslims-officials-1629446-2019-12-18.

8. Poddar, M. 2016. 'The Citizenship (Amendment) Bill, 2016: International Law on Religion-Based Discrimination and Naturalisation Law', *Indian Law Review*, 2(1): 108–118.

9. https://thelogicalindian.com/fact-check/delhi-police-fire-bus

10. Ranjan, A. 2019. 'National Register of Citizen Update: History and Its Impact', *Asian Ethnicity*, pp. 1–17. Available at DOI: 10.1080/14631369.2019.1629274.

11. https://www.indianbarassociation.org/indias-refugee-policy/

12. https://www.youtube.com/watch?v=IL8i4XiLEkc

13. Tripathi, R. 2019. 'Citizenship Amendment Act Decoded: What It Holds for India', *The Economic Times*, 23 December. Available at https://economictimes.indiatimes.com/news/politics-and-nation/citizenship-amendment-bill-decoded-what-it-holds-for-india/articleshow/72466056.cms (accessed on 10 May 2020).

14. https://www.newindianexpress.com/nation/2018/sep/20/cpim-opposes-triple-talaq-ordinance-says-its-undemocratic-1874865.html

FOUR

THE PRELUDE:
VIOLENCE IN UNIVERSITIES

Introduction

The CAB 2019 received assent from the president of India on 12 December 2019 and became an Act. The CAA came into force on 10 January 2020. Between these two dates, i.e., 12 December 2019 and 10 January 2020, four public university campuses in India—JMI, DU and JNU in Delhi, and Aligarh Muslim University (AMU) in Aligarh, UP—saw violent protests. Initially centred on the CAA, these protests eventually became sites for mobilisation along a distinct Left–Jihadi ideological pattern. This chapter examines these university protests in detail.

Jamia Millia Islamia (JMI) and Aligarh Muslim University (AMU)

Both Jamia Millia Islamia (JMI) and Aligarh Muslim University(AMU) have a long history, tracing back to colonial India. The AMU had originated as Madarsatul Uloom, a seminary, in 1875 and evolved into the Muhammadan Anglo Oriental College. In 1920, the Indian Legislative Council set up AMU and all the assets of the college were thus transferred to it.[1] JMI was set up by Hakim Ajmal Khan and prominent philanthropists in 1920. In 1988, it became a central university by an Act of parliament.[2] Both institutions are funded by the central government and are designated as 'minority institutions'.

Likewise, DU, too, is a centrally funded University with a number of constituent affiliated colleges.

Large-scale violence in JMI and AMU started on 15 December 2019. Three days prior, on 12 December, an anti-CAA programme was organised in AMU in which Yogendra Yadav, a former member of AAP, too had addressed the gathering.[3] The very next day, on 13 December 2019, anti-CAA protest marches were organised by AMU's students and teachers.

There was similar tension at the JMI campus as well. Having dissenting views or holding peaceful protests on any issue is not a new thing in any university. However, whatever happened on 15 December 2019 at the Jamia campus made it a black Sunday. It was on this day that violence occurred at two places in the neighbouring area of New Friends Colony, as well as outside and inside the campus.

The Manifestation and Sequence of the Violence

A few hundred anti-CAA protesters had gathered at the anti-CAA protest organised outside the JMI gate on 15 December 2019. The protest was characterised by speeches and sloganeering. The area member of the legislative assembly (MLA) from AAP, Amanatullah Khan too addressed the protesters in Jamia Nagar less than two kilometres from the gates of JMI.[4]

His speeches on that day were extremely provocative. He referred to communal riots since 1947 claiming that Muslim suffered the brunt of the violence. He claimed that had Muslims come on the streets in earlier episodes of communal violence, subsequent episodes would not have happened. He was heard asking the crowd to reflect on the reasons why Muslims who ruled India for a thousand years were now paupers. He further claimed that it was getting difficult for Muslims in India to live, wear their traditional clothes, protect places of worship. Distorted facts were shared about the CAA and the

Muslim community was made to believe that the newly passed legislation was against them and their citizenship. Violence broke out in a five kilometres radius of his speech. Meanwhile, a crowd had also come out on roads from nearby Jamia Nagar. It gathered on the New Friends Colony Road, a residential colony in the vicinity. All of a sudden the crowd became aggressive as it shouted anti-CAA and azadi slogans. They had stones and sticks in their hands. It was apparent that the crowd was not there for a peaceful protest but with the intention of inciting violence. Arson and vandalism continued as their numbers kept on swelling. The crowd set ablaze four public buses and many private vehicles. The fire tender vehicle and the personnel who came to extinguish the fire were attacked and injured. It was a huge crowd and it could not be ascertained whether they were students or outsiders. Some of the rioters had masked their faces.[5] They were freely roaming on the colony road and were creating mayhem. They targeted public buses, private vehicles and police vehicles too. The road was blocked and traffic could not move. The passengers travelling in buses were scared. Some videos with vandalised buses and broken windows were also shared in the media.

Outside the university gate too, the protesters became aggressive and violent. They started pelting stones at police personnel. As in Friends Colony, here, too, the police fired tear-gas shells and the crowd was baton-charged to make it disperse. Some people from the crowd picked up tear-gas shells from the road and hurled them back at the police. As the police tried to nab them, instead of retreating, they ran inside the campus. Some of the stone-pelting crowd was already inside the campus. As the police followed them inside, they tried to run away in different directions. A majority of them ran towards the university's library, the Dr Zakir Husain Library. The police followed them and in the course of trying to nab them, lathi charged them there.

This is the entire sequence of events as it happened in Jamia on 15 December 2019. Police action led to media speculations that the police had entered the Jamia campus by force and lathi charged the students. It was projected that the police assaulted innocent students sitting and studying in the library. However, after around a month of the incident, in mid-January, the police and media outlets came out with video footage from inside and outside the Jamia campus that pointed to a different reality. The videos had the date and time marked on them as they were collected from CCTV footage from multiple locations. Meanwhile, a tussle between the university administration and the police was reported over handing over the footage to the police department. However, some media houses shared multiple videos to establish the facts of the 15 December incidents for the time between 4.30pm to 6.30pm.

The dots were joined and eventually, the design came out. It also offered the police some proof to corroborate what it had been claiming regarding the reason for their entry into the campus. They had been saying that the aim of the forces was chasing the rioters and trying to nab them. The videos showed that a crowd gathered at the Jamia gate at 4.56pm. In a few seconds, they entered the campus. This was a crowd that included some masked men. After about 10 minutes, at 5.10pm, they were seen pelting stones at the police from inside the campus. The police fired tear-gas shells. Some of the rioters picked up the shells and hurled them back at the police personnel. At around 6pm, a huge crowd gathered at gate number 4 of the university and attacked the police with stones. At the same time, some masked men were seen roaming around inside the campus. They blocked the police from entering and continued pelting stones. At 6.20pm, a huge crowd gathered at the gate and entered the campus, and was followed by the police who were seen chasing them. While some of the rioters retreated into the campus, others ran in different directions with the cops on their heels. They entered the Dr Zakir Husain

Library; this crowd also included some masked men. It is at this point, inside the library that the police lathi charged them; this portion of the video, of around 23 seconds, had been shared widely by the protesters and media. Another CCTV video showed a huge stone being broken into smaller pieces to be hurled at the police.

It was proved that rioters had taken shelter in the university library which had led police to take action. They had indulged in violence and arson and came inside the university to hide, pretending to be students and escape a crackdown. As their identities were verified on the basis of videos, many of them turned out to be outsiders. None among the 10 who were arrested by the police was a student.

The police claimed that the violence was not spontaneous but was well planned. The protesters/rioters had the intention to be aggressive. The MoS (Home), G. Kishan Reddy, stated in the Lok Sabha that the Jamia violence led to the injury of 62 police personnel and 127 other people including students. Four public buses were torched and some police vehicles vandalised and torched. Traffic was disrupted, including metro services on the route.

This is what he mentioned in his written reply to Lok Sabha:

As reported by Delhi Police, they entered the University Campus chasing the violent congregation of students/ mob, to nab/ disperse the offenders, control the situation and to protect the Government property as well as saving the lives of innocent students residing in the Campus area.[6]

Some political leaders and persons associated with some organisations were named in the charge-sheet filed by the Delhi police in February 2020. Delhi's AAP MLA, Amanatullah Khan, was alleged to have addressed a huge gathering and incited the crowd. Violence allegedly began immediately after this speech. While Khan had given his speech in Shaheen Bagh, he had been active in various points in Jamia Nagar on 15

December 2019. The resulting violence radiated out to many points in the area.

The names of other people who were alleged to have incited protesters were local youth leader Ashu Khan; former Congress MLA, Asif Khan; Karim Usman from Chhatra Yuva Sangharsh Samiti (CYSS), the student body of AAP; Chandan Kumar from the All-India Students' Association (AISA) and others. Later on, Sharjeel Imam, a PhD student from JNU, was also booked for his inflammatory speeches at Jamia and later at AMU, as well as distributing pamphlets with distorted facts in mosques on 14 and 15 December. His speech at AMU to block the 'chicken neck' of India (the North-East) from the rest of the country mirrored a battle cry often advanced by foreign powers for the dismemberment of India. More than an hour after the violent protests in the Jamia vicinity ended, AMU students started a protest outside their campus, to show that they stood in solidarity with Jamia 'students'. The protesters broke the police cordon and the same pattern of stone pelting was followed in AMU too. The police, too, responded, firing tear-gas shells to disperse the crowd.[7]

However, in AMU, contrary to the Jamia incident, the police had entered the campus after it received the request to do so from the university authorities. The police had followed a standard operating procedure in the case. They claimed to have been forced to use mild baton charging to disperse the violent crowd.

The Urban Naxal Organisational Networks and Their Responses

As per the Urban Naxal manual on work in urban areas, a number of front organisations, youth and cultural groups, human rights fronts have been created by Maoist organisations in urban areas in the past few decades. Many of these organisations have networks that feed into universities and colleges. This is in line with the 'Strategy and Tactics of the Indian Revolution' document outlining the theoretical design of the Maoists for an Indian communist revolution. This document clearly explains that Urban Naxalism has roots not only in universities but also in the media and among the police and lawyers. This is the network that got activated after the violence in Jamia and AMU.

Articles were written in the national as well as international media to internationalise the issue in a two-pronged manner—one, that an anti-Muslim law had been passed in India and second, that the state police under the Hindutva Modi government had attacked innocent students in universities. That the central government was exercising violence against minorities became the headlines. 'India Police Storms Jamia', was the headline on 16 December 2019 of a news report on the Al Jazeera website.[8]

The focus remained on how the 'anti-student', 'anti-people' government had illegally entered the university campus and used aggression to terrorise hapless students. It was projected that the right to protest was being crushed through brutal assaults. A planned attack on education was taking place to silence people who held a different view from that of the government. Selective videos were shared to set the larger narrative. As mentioned in the previous section, an edited 23-second video of footage inside the Dr Zakir Husain Library in Jamia Milia Islamia was first shared which showed police lathi charging 'students' sitting in the reading hall of the library.

While the violence in Jamia and AMU was clearly street violence that could have been a grave public law and order issue, groups allied to Communist parties organised and mobilised an emergency protest demonstration for Jamia students at the Delhi police headquarters, at ITO at 9pm on the same night. Social media was used extensively to mobilise the students from AISA, Students' Federation of India (SFI) and other such politically affiliated students' groups, as well as the faculty of DU, JNU, JMI, Ambedkar University and civil society members who were similarly aligned.

Facebook and WhatsApp were used extensively to create stories of police brutality and also to somehow link the police department with parties and groups affiliated to the central government. This was a common strategy, seen very often in these protests and the next few months held what can only be called 'Facebook and WhatsApp kangaroo courts'. Facebook profiles of students belonging to the Akhil Bharatiya Vidyarthi Parishad (ABVP), the student's wing of the BJP, would be picked up, with the display picture circled. This would be superimposed with the face of a member of the police personnel claiming that the ruling party had infiltrated police ranks.[9] University faculty members and students who did not agree with anti-CAA positions were hounded and singled out.[10]

Many WhatsApp groups, Facebook pages and Twitter handles were created instantly. Several rumours and fake news related to the CAA and NRC, in addition to lies related to incidents in Jamia, were shared to instigate and mobilise. Hate messages were created and circulated.

On the night of 15 December, a message was shared that a boy named Shakeel had been killed by the cops in the JMI campus. It was later revealed that this news was fake. The forthcoming assembly elections on 8 February in Delhi made things worse as political parties pitched in to use the Jamia incidence to their advantage. The Delhi deputy chief minister Manish Sisodia shared a very irresponsible tweet on Twitter on 15 December 2019, claiming that public buses torched by rioters were set ablaze by the police itself. He added that the Delhi police was working on behest of the BJP (the ruling political party at the centre). AAP members Atishi Marlena and Sanjay Singh, too, shared the same video. It was later found that this was a fake narrative possibly manufactured to demonise the Delhi police and the ruling party at the centre.

This fake narrative was busted the very next day when the bus was seen intact.

The Nature of Political Mobilisation in the Anti-CAA Violence

On the night of 15 December itself, 'Rise in Rage' programmes were organized by organisations that largely fall under the Left-Trade union spectrum. It has already been mentioned that the JNU Students' Union (JNUSU) issued a statement appealing everyone to reach the police headquarters at 9pm on 15 December 2019 at ITO. A number of other pre-existing umbrella organisations like All India Save Education issued statements against the Jamia incident.[11] The cadre of this umbrella organization comprises activists from the Students Federation of India (SFI), Birsa Ambedkar Phule Students' Association (BAPSA) and other communist organisations. A social media campaign with the hashtag #shutdowncapital was launched.

Another umbrella organisation, the National Alliance of People's Movements (NAPM) issued press statements against the Jamia violence. The ideological spectrum of organisations under this umbrella is largely communist. It has a clear stand against the BJP, the Rashtriya Swayamsevak Sangh (RSS) and whoever falls under their definition of fascist. This organisation had also written a lot against the Ayodhya case judgement and called it an assault on the secular fabric of the Constitution.[12]

NAPM had been active in anti-CAA programmes in Mumbai, Shimla, Dharmshala, the Lal Qila to Shaheed Park March on 19 December 2019, the Preamble reading at India Gate on 16 December 2019, the protest against the Jamia, AMU police violence at Lucknow, the Rise in Rage Protest against the attack on students and faculty of Jamia and AMU and some more. On the same night of 15 December 2019, the Delhi Minorities Commission sought information of victims of protests. A complaint was filed with the National Human Rights Commission (NHRC) against the Delhi police. Meanwhile, support from Oxford and Harvard University was also arranged.[13] For a few days, stories of Jamia violence and police brutality and the narrative of how innocent students were targeted went around in the national and international media. Much was written and said on how it was an attack on the autonomy of a university, on intellectual free space, etc.

Apart from the left spectrum, the CYSS, the student wing of AAP, was also active in campus protests initially. There were a number of political activists of the Congress Party who were also a regular part of anti-CAA protests in December 2019 and thereafter.[14]

Ironically, a few days later, on 5 January 2020, when violence broke out in the JNU campus, the Delhi police did not enter the premises as it waited for permission from the JNU administration. The same network that questioned the police in the case of Jamia and AMU was now asking the Delhi police why they waited for JNU administration's permission to enter the campus.

The legal position on police action in university campuses is very clear. Law enforcement agencies including the police are empowered to enter any public space where there is violation of law and danger to public peace. All sections of the Indian Penal Code (IPC) are valid on university campuses and other educational spaces. However, the police department typically coordinates this action with university and college administrations as a matter of mutual respect and understanding.[15]

The violence in January in JNU was also an outcome of the sustained hysteria around the CAA and over a fee rationalisation in the university. Predictably, the violence caused an escalation of the hysteria in Urban Naxal networks, ranging from affiliated political parties to the judiciary and ex-bureaucrats. The Left-aligned media also called it the 'night of long rods'[16] in an attempt to somehow bring in the fascist regime narrative.

Action at Courts

The network of Urban Naxalism uses the legal system primarily in the form of human rights activism and the civil liberties spectrum. This is in keeping with the larger theory of Urban Naxalism elaborated in previous chapters. On the legal front, Prashant Bhushan, Indira Jaisingh and other advocates filed six petitions in the Supreme Court on 16 December 2019. However, the Supreme Court asked the petitioners to approach respective high courts of their jurisdiction. CJI Bobde stated:

Supreme Court is not the place to establish facts.... Go to the Courts where you can establish facts. We are not a trial Court. We will not be establishing facts. You should be knowing this. Why were we approached...? If buses have been burnt, why will FIRs not to be filed?[17]

The Delhi High Court was then approached to seek interim relief from judicial arrests in the cases related to the violence on the Jamia campus, but the high court did not pronounce any interim relief. A petition was also filed in the Allahabad High Court to investigate the AMU anti-CAA violence through the formation of a court-monitored committee. The case was listed for 2 January 2020. However, the high court did not pass any order on the petition. On 6 January, the court directed the NHRC to probe into the AMU incidence of violence and submit a report by 17 February 2020.

The NHRC recommended action against policemen and on the basis of this recommendation, the Allahabad High Court ordered the university, the police and the state government to submit a compliance report by 25 March 2020. A petition was filed by the registrar of Jamia Millia as well. The Delhi police submitted in the court that it was constrained to enter the campus to contain violence, protect and rescue innocent students and ensure normalcy. The affidavit mentioned that the police, being a professional force, showed maximum restraint and, despite provocation by the protesters, used minimum force.

The police also submitted that local leaders and politicians had instigated the protesters who were armed with lathis, stones, petrol bombs, and tube lights. The intentions from the very beginning were not those of a peaceful protest. The police further stated that it tried to disperse the crowds but instead, in what seemed like a strategy, the protesters entered the campus to use it as a shield. Before entering the campus, the police kept making announcements from loudspeakers to maintain law and order but the unruly mob did not pay any attention to it. They entered the campus and started pelting stones, tube lights, etc. Meanwhile, the matter in Delhi High Court was to be heard on 7 April 2020.

One petition was filed by an injured JMI student, asking for compensation. The court set 27 May 2020 as a deadline for the Delhi police, the Delhi government and the centre to submit their report.

The Role of the PFI and Radical Fundamentalist Muslim Groups in the Violence on Campuses

According to police reports, 150 PFI members had arrived in the Jamia area two days before the violence and had an active role in the violence on 15 December 2019 in the Jamia university vicinity. It has also been reported in the media that some PFI offices have opened up in the vicinity of Shaheen Bagh in recent years and their activities increased considerably in the lead up to the anti-CAA protests in the area.

On 23 December 2019, the UP police arrested the PFI's UP head, Waseem, the treasurer, Ashfaq and another member, Nadeem.

The Enforcement Directorate (ED) has made startling claims that PFI provided Rs120 crore financial support to fund the anti-CAA protests. It has been reported that bank accounts of certain senior advocates have had direct transfers of money from the PFI. Later it was revealed that this is indeed the case in previous lawsuits being fought by these advocates.

It has been mentioned previously that some of the slogans which were raised at the protest sites of both the campuses, like 'Naara e takbeer, Allah hu Akbar' (The slogan of Takbir—Allah is greatest) and 'Tera mera rishta kya, la ilaha illallah' (What is the relationship between you and me, that of the belief that there is no God but Allah) are part of the Islamic Shahada, which is the Muslim declaration of faith in Allah. Further slogans like 'Hinduon se azadi' (Freedom from Hindus), 'Hindutva se azadi' (Freedom from Hindutva), etc., had nothing to do with the Constitution or the CAA.

Action by the University Administration

The chief proctor of JMI, Waseem Ahmad Khan, issued a statement that the police had entered the campus forcefully and had attacked the students and the staff.

'Police entered the campus by force, no permission was taken. Staff members and students were beaten up and forced to leave the campus,' the chief proctor said.[18]

The agitating students surrounded vice chancellor Najma Akhtar's office, demanding the registration of an FIR against the Delhi police in connection with the violence on the campus. Akhtar told the students that the process to register an FIR will begin. 'Don't ask me exact dates. When I said today that FIR will happen, that means it will happen,' she said.[19]

The vice chancellor confirmed the entry of outsiders into the campus as she reported that 750 fake identity cards were recovered from the campus. This also corroborates the police claim that all the 10 protesters/rioters arrested by the police were 'outsiders'.

After the news of the police attack on Jamia Millia students started filtering over social media, AMU students came out spontaneously in solidarity. In the evening, the students started gathering at the library canteen and moved towards the main gate, Bab-e-Syed, where most of the protests usually take place. The administration called for the police in view of the tension and violence on the campus happening in the university. A heavy contingent of police, supported by the Rapid Action Force (RAF), was thus deployed. The police confronted the protesters and the students were forced back into their hostels. Internet services were suspended. After the 15 December incident, the administration suspended classes and examinations till 5 January 2020. Later, the hostels were asked to be vacated. The AMU proctor, Professor Afifullah Khan said that some security personnel had been injured in stone-pelting near the gate. The AMU administration put up notices refraining students from taking part in any protests within 100 metres of the campus. A one-man judicial enquiry was set up by the university administration under V.K. Gupta, former chief justice of the Jharkhand High Court to investigate.

Out of the 26 persons arrested in connection with AMU violence, only 8 were students while the others were outsiders. According to the police, 1,000 students were booked for the 15 December violence at AMU and were charged under various sections of the Indian Penal Code (IPC).

Conclusion

The sequence of events that started at the universities to mobilise and instigate crowds through religious polarisation by playing the minority and the victim cards, and the effort to discredit the police were early moves in a carefully crafted strategy. It unfolded subsequently in the high media visibility and Constitution-spouting phase of the strategy that was seen at the protest sites at Shaheen Bagh and other places that came up immediately thereafter, and are dealt with in detail in the next chapter. One will see how the strategy changed and shifted to bring in Urban Naxal–Jihadi elements, tried to build a larger constituency using art and other elements, swore allegiance to constitutional values but articulated hatred and polarisation. While the sites remained university inspired, the tactics had changed. Anti-CAA hysteria was built by instigating a fear psychosis among the minority community. The link with the Delhi elections that were about a month away at that time is something that can easily be inferred. This second phase of entrenched protest sites was to ultimately give way to the Delhi riots at the end of February, which will also be examined in a subsequent chapter in detail. The unfolding of the strategy and its regrettable outcome is a sad commentary on the way the Urban Naxal–Jihadi elements operate to further their ends.

References

1. For an interesting and concise history of the AMU, see Noorani, A.G. 2016. 'History of Aligarh Muslim University', *Frontline*, 13 May. Available at https://frontline.thehindu.com/the-nation/history-of-aligarh-muslim-university/article8523802.ece.

2. For details on JMI, see https://www.jmi.ac.in/upload/jamiadocs/JAMIA/minorityinstitution.pdf.

3. Mishra, Suchita. 2019. 'Yogendra Yadav Calls for AMU Students to Launch Agitation to Repeal Citizenship Amendment Bill', *Patrika*, 13 December. Available at https://www.patrika.com/aligarh-news/yogendra-yadav-call-on-amu-students-to-build-big-movement-against-cab-5499438/.

4. To hear part of Amanatullah Khan's 15 December 2019 speech, see https://youtu.be/C3U3C-goUGY.

5. Online Desk. 2019. 'Anti-CAA Stir: Violence Rocks South Delhi, Buses Torched, Nearly 60 Injured', *The New Indian Express*, 15 December. Available at https://www.newindianexpress.com/cities/delhi/2019/dec/15/anti-citizenship-act-stir-violent-protests-rock-jamia-buses-burnt-tear-gas-fired-2076511.html.

6. The Leaflet News. 2020. 'Jamia Violence: A Total of 15 People Arrested by Delhi Police', *The Leaflet*, 4 February. Available at

https://theleaflet.in/jamia-violence-a-total-of-15-people-arrested-by-delhi-police/.

7. India Today Web Desk. 2019. 'CAA Protest at AMU Turns Violent, Internet Suspended, University Shut', *India Today*, 15 December. Available at https://www.indiatoday.in/india/story/caa-protest-police-uses- tear-gas-after-amu-students-pelt-stones-1s628511-2019-12-15 (accessed on 21 May 2020).

8. Al Jazeera News. 2019. 'India Police Storm Jamia, AMU to Break Citizenship Law Protests', *Al Jazeera*, 16 December. Available at https://www.aljazeera.com/news/2019/12/dozens-injured-india-police-storm-universities-191216033648272.html#:~:text=More%20than%20100%20students%20have,holding%20anti%2Dcitizenship%20law%20protests (accessed on 22 May 2020).

9. Chandra, Divya. 2019. 'Man in Civilian Clothes Is Delhi Cop, Not ABVP's Bharat Sharma', *The Quint*. Available at https://www.thequint.com/news/webqoof/did-abvp-member-attack-protesting-students-disguised-as-cop-fact-check.

10. For an understanding of the kangaroo courts operational in Left-dominated institutions, see India Today Web Desk. 'Traitors of JNU, Architects of Violence: Poster at University Blames Profs, Chief Proctor for Jan 5 Incident', *India Today*. Available at https://www.indiatoday.in/india/story/jnu-posters-january-5-violence-assistant-professors-chief-proctor-blamed-1635943-2020-01-11. The standard strategy to intimidate is to link any dissenting voice with the RSS. A virtual death sentence is then passed.

11. Sabrang. 2019. 'All India Forum of Save Education Condemns the Barbaric Act by Delhi Police on the Students of Jamia', *Sabrang*, 16 December. Available at https://www.sabrangindia.in/ann/all-india-forum-save-education-condemns-barbaric-act-delhi-police-students-jamia.

12. For further insights on the National Alliance People's Movement (NAPM), see http://napm-india.org/ideology/.

13. PTI. 2019. 'From Harvard to Oxford, Universities Abroad See Protests against Police Crackdown in Jamia, AMU', *The Economic Times*, 17 December. Available at https://economictimes.indiatimes.com/news/politics-and-nation/ from-oxford-to-harvard-universities-abroad-see-protests-against-police-crackdown-in-jamia-amu/articleshow/72839850.cms (accessed on 25 May 2020).

14. IANS. 2019. 'Anti-CAA Protest: Ex-MLA, AISA, AAP Student Leaders in Jamia Violence FIR', ABP News, 18 December. Available at https://news.abplive.com/news/india/anti-caa-protest-ex-mla-aisa-aap-student-leaders-in-jamia-violence-fir-1126993.
15. Mohanty, Kenneth (Times News Network). 2020. 'Do Police Need Permission to Enter Campuses', The Times of India, 12 February. Available at https://timesofindia.indiatimes.com/india/do-police-need-to-worry-about-permission-to-enter-campuses/articleshow/73242855.cms.
16. For an understanding of the parallel, see 'The Night of Long Knives', The Weiner Holocaust Library. Available at https://www.theholocaustexplained.org/the-nazi-rise-to-power/ how-did-the-nazi-gain-power/night-of-long-knives/.
17. Nagpal, Deepak. 2019. 'Won't Intervene; Approach High Courts: Supreme Court to Petitioners in Jamia Violence Case', Times Now News, 17 December. Available at https://www.timesnownews.com/india/article/won-t-intervene-approach-high-courts-supreme-court-to-petitioners-in-jamia-violence-case/528309.
18. PTI. 2019. 'Police Entered Campus by Force, No Permission Taken: Jamia Millia Islamia Chief Proctor', The Economic Times, 16 December. Available at https://economictimes.indiatimes.com/news/politics-and-nation/police-entered-campus-by-force-no-permission-taken-jamia-millia-islamia-chief-proctor/articleshow/72691773.cms (accessed on 26 May 2020).
19. Sarfaraz, Kainat. 2020. 'Jamia Vice Chancellor Reaches Out to Protesting Students, Makes a Promise on FIR against Cops', Hindustan Times, 13 January. Available at https://www.hindustantimes.com/delhi-news/jamia-vice-chancellor-reaches-out-to-protesting-students-makes-a-promise- on-fir-against-cops/story-RD7uPnSaYrseNncazycwPO.html (accessed on 26 May 2020).

FIVE

THE INTERLUDE:
THE SHAHEEN BAGH MODEL

Introduction

The first phase of the events could be observed in university campuses at AMU, JMI, JNU and DU on 15 December 2019. Large-scale street rioting by crowds comprising students and local elements led to severe police action. This was followed by the second phase that is the establishment of Shaheen Bagh and other protest sites all across Delhi. The activity at these protest sites continued till 15 February 2020. This chapter looks at this interregnum between the establishment of these sites and the eruption of violence in North East Delhi. Anti-CAA protest sites entered a different phase of activity from the last week of January to the last week of February. This was a phase when these sites all over Delhi were cultivated into sites of division. A well-networked, university-based Urban Naxal–Jihadi network spread out into these areas. Their allied organisations and individuals ranging from artists to poets used the anti-CAA protest sites to drum up anti-government, anti-Hindu hysteria.

This was also the phase in which elections in Delhi were held. The effects of election campaigning and the role of the dharna sites therein will be examined in detail. This was also the time when anti-CAA election speeches made by leaders of political parties outside Delhi impacted the atmosphere of the Delhi assembly elections.

State Assembly Elections in Delhi

Elections to the state assembly in Delhi were announced on 6 January. Since 2014, elections in Delhi have been a high-octane battle between the BJP, the INC and the AAP. In 2015, AAP had won 67 out of 70 seats, 3 seats going to the BJP. Congress could not open its account. Regarding issues in 2020 elections, apart from the smog, dirty water, very bad sewage system, overpopulated Delhi, 'Shaheen Bagh' became a major poll issue. Since 15 December 2019, i.e., after the CAA was passed by both the houses of parliament, Shaheen Bagh became the major site for protest against this law. It was a long-drawn-out protest with its share of fame and discredit.

The fact that the anti-CAA protests and Shaheen Bagh were to be pitched as a Hindu–Muslim issue became evident when videos of Amanatullah Khan, AAP MLA from the Okhla constituency, of which Shaheen Bagh is a part, went viral on social media. In these videos, he was seen inciting the Muslims gathered, in the Okhla area in large numbers with claims that, after CAA, Modi will not allow Muslims to wear skull caps or keep beards. There will be a ban on the burkha. There will be no permission for the azan in mosques to be heard over loudspeakers and no allowances for mikes. He was also caught on camera saying that Muslims have ruled India for a thousand years.[1] A complaint was also filed against him for inciting the public to violence and vandalism.

Waris Pathan, the All-India Majlis-e-Ittahadul Muslimeen (AIMIM) leader from Maharashtra, made a speech in Karnataka, saying that even though there were only 15 crore Muslims, they could overpower the 100 crore Hindus. The BJP was equated with Hindu and the AAP with a party for Muslims.[2]

That vote-bank politics was being played out on the pretext of CAA and Shaheen Bagh was the election pitch taken by the BJP. Prime Minister Modi, during the election campaign, said that Shaheen Bagh was an 'experiment' which was particularly designed to destroy the Nation's harmony. The party firmly took the stand that the Shaheen Bagh and anti-CAA protests were being manipulated by rival parties to create and deepen a social fault line in Delhi.[3]

This war was fought across all fronts, including very vigorously on social media platforms such as Facebook, WhatsApp, Twitter and several others. This was the pitch occupied by Anurag Thakur, Yogi Adityanath, Parvesh Verma and Home Minister Amit Shah.

Sonia Gandhi and Congress leaders were seen addressing people and telling them that it was their last chance to come out on the streets and capture public areas. She called it as an 'aar-paar ki ladai' (a fight to the finish).[4]

In a tweet, Congress leader Rahul Gandhi said: 'It's not good enough just to feel for India. At times like these, it's critical to show that you're Indian and won't allow India to be destroyed by hatred.' Rahul Gandhi said, 'Don't be afraid. Congress party is with you'.[5] Mani Shankar Aiyar, another Congress leader, without naming anyone, said, 'I am ready for whatever sacrifices that need to be made. We will see whose hands are stronger, ours or that killer's [referring to Modi and Amit Shah]'.[6]

'Attack on students is a blot on the nation,' Shashi Tharoor remarked in the media, showing his support for anti-CAA Protests at Jamia and Shaheen Bagh.[7] People in the film industry also joined the wagon of hatemongers. Bollywood actress Swara Bhaskar gave statements like 'Government fuels hatred in society'. She came out in favour of Shaheen Bagh, saying on camera that uniformed men had been looting and killing unarmed Muslims.[8]

Left activist Harsh Mander addressed a crowd at Jamia saying that they had no faith in the Supreme Court as it had not upheld the ideals of secularism in case of recent judgements like Article 370, triple talaq, Ram Janmabhoomi, etc. It seems as though courts and the parliament cannot decide these issues. They have to be decided on the streets.[9]

Videos of small kids surfaced, where they were shown saying things about Modi and Amit Shah: 'Woh hamein desh se nikaal denge ... hamein detention camp mein bhej denge' (The prime minister and the home minister will throw us out of the country ... and will send us to detention camps). Many such videos showed children raising azadi slogans, even saying 'Tera baap bhi dega azadi' (a disrespectful colloquialism that roughly translates to even your father will give us freedom). Visuals of several children being present at these protests were seen on social media. Parents and organisers of these protests and rallies dragged children (who were unaware about agitations) to these manifestations. Even the children's rights body, the National Commission or Protection of Child Rights (NCPCR) took cognisance of the matter and issued an order to the district magistrate of the area to identify the children and send them for counselling.[10]

These videos were widely circulated on social media and also covered in primetime debates by the mainstream media. Rhetoric and the blame game were at an all-time high. Videos and interviews also showed that the protesting women knew nothing about the CAA or the NRC. They had been told that this law was anti-Muslim and that all Muslims would have to leave the country if they could not prove their citizenship. No effort was made to educate them as to what the law was about and who it was for.

Arvind Kejriwal, being the clever politician that he is, proved smarter and changed his strategy for the Delhi elections. He knew that taking sides on the Shaheen Bagh issue will be suicidal for him. Thus, he avoided this controversy. He downplayed the statement of his deputy chief minister, who had spoken in support of Shaheen Bagh. He, in fact, largely avoided the issue and even when forced to make a statement, said that it was largely an issue of the union government.

Kejriwal stopped attacking Modi, the union government, the Election Commission, the lieutenant governor, electronic voting machines (EVMs), etc. He stopped spitting venom at them. He projected himself as the son of Delhi who was always available. He announced freebies—free water, electricity, bus rides, sewage connection, *teerth yatras*, etc., for the people in Delhi. He steered clear of the Shaheen Bagh issue by neither commenting on it nor visiting it. In fact, he cleverly told the voters that they voted for Modi in the general elections but he had full faith that they will vote for his party in the Delhi assembly elections. While his party's MLAs were polarising Muslim votes for him, he started going to temples to garner the Hindu votes, even reciting the *Hanuman Chalisa* on one of the TV channels. He played safe and used the victim card sometimes.[11]

This strategy worked. Amanatullah Khan, the candidate from his party from Shaheen Bagh area, won with a very high margin of over 70,000 votes. AAP won 62 out of 70 seats in Delhi, with BJP winning 8 seats.[12] The Congress neither focused on the national nor the local issues. They never put up a fight and seemed to be less interested in winning itself and more interested in ensuring a defeat for the BJP. It only put up some banners and posters that focused on the past glory under Sheila Dikshit, the late former chief minister of Delhi from the Congress.

Thus, while the BJP highlighted the dangerous experiment of Shaheen Bagh, Congress leaders called these anti-CAA protests 'aar-paar ki ladai'. Kejriwal strategically underplayed it while his MLAs like Amanatullah Khan and others spread hate and polarised the city. It is imperative to understand that the anti-CAA protests had an important impact on the Delhi elections.

The Establishment and the Spread of the Shaheen Bagh Protest Site

Shaheen Bagh is a recent establishment in the maze of small colonies that comprise Jamia Nagar. Settled in 1985 from plots sold by the Hindu Gujjar community who owned agricultural land here, the area rapidly became a Muslim-majority one. Eighty bhigas (approximately 32 acres) of land was purchased by Shariq Ansarullah, who settled and named this area after a poem by Allama Iqbal, the spiritual founder of Pakistan. Ansarullah originally belongs to Rampur in UP. Hindus and some Sikhs who owned land here shifted out rapidly after the demolition of the Babri Masjid in 1992. Now the area has a mixed population, with a majority of the residents being Muslim. Many of them are students and teachers in neighbouring Jamia. Other than this, there are white-collar workers, shop owners and self-employed persons. Broadly, Shaheen Bagh can be characterised as a Muslim working-class neighbourhood. And it was established as a protest site on 15 December 2019, after the violence in JMI on the same day.

The Blockage of Roads

The protesters at Shaheen Bagh blocked two carriageways on the GD Birla Road, a significant arterial road, disrupting a major entry point to the Kalindi Kunj Bridge. The 150-metre-wide protest site included tents on one side, with the other side reinforced with grilles. Five barricades were placed by the police in the area subsequently, in the backdrop of firing by a man near the protest site at the beginning of February. A visit to the site shows that these barricades were absolutely valid to prevent utter chaos on Madanpur Khadar Road and the Mithapur–Molarband Road, which are smaller roads that carry huge traffic. The opening up of one carriageway was also not an option since this would lead to possible clashes and accidents, with protesters out on the road. Given that the

Shaheen Bagh protest site occupied a major arterial road, there was significant inconvenience to the public and emerged as a major law and order problem in the area.

Barricades were placed near the Okhla Bird Sanctuary (carriageway heading towards Delhi), the roundabout near the Kalindi Kunj Metro Station, on Kalindi Kunj Bridge (towards Delhi), Amrapali Road, GD Birla Marg (on both carriageways), Vishwasji Sadak (on both carriageways) and the loop near Apollo Hospital. As a result, traffic coming from Apollo Hospital towards Noida, from Faridabad towards Noida and from Noida towards Sarita Vihar in South Delhi had to face diversions. The Delhi Noida Direct (DND) Flyway, Mathura Road and Akshardham Road had become the alternate routes where commuters faced heavy jams during peak hours and slow vehicular movement the entire day.

Many times, affected locals would come out to protest in large numbers due to the daily frustration and disruption of their lives. The matter also reached the Supreme Court, which then appointed interlocutors to talk to the Shaheen Bagh protesters. Meanwhile, the daily grind for the locals continued

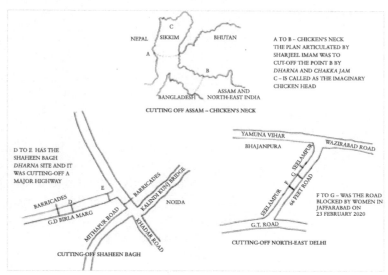

until eventually, the police cleared the road due to the Covid-19 pandemic and the subsequent lockdown.

The Women and Grandmothers of Shaheen Bagh

Tactically, women rapidly took the centre stage at Shaheen Bagh. The homemakers from the area formed the core of the protesting crowd, becoming the front lines of the protest and the faces for media interaction. The women came along with children of all ages. Female students also formed a part of the protesting crowds. High visibility was ensured by the protestors for some of the women, like Sarwari, 75, Bilkis, 82 and Noor Nisha, 75, who came to be known as Shaheen Bagh ki dadiyan (grandmothers of Shaheen Bagh). With elections in Delhi looming, Shaheen Bagh became a focal point for media attention. The public of the area, however, did not manage to get relief either from the government, law enforcement agencies or the courts.

The Spread of the Network to Other Areas

Shaheen Bagh provided the template for similar protests at other sites in Delhi. On 19 December 2019, protests by women were initiated at the Seelampur Metro Station. As a result, entrance to seven metro stations in the area, including Seelampur, were closed—Johri Enclave, Shiv Vihar, Jaffrabad, Maujpur–Babarpur, Gokulpuri and Welcome. On 20 December 2019, another protest site was established under the Inderlok Metro Station. And on the same day, a crowd of almost 40,000 Muslims came out on Road Number 66 in Jaffrabad at 2.30am. This crowd was dispersed by the Delhi police with the help of the local ulema. Seelampur remained tense, with drones used for maintaining vigil. On 27 December 2019, the NIA busted an ISIS module in Seelampur.

On 13 January 2020, anti-CAA protest sites were established at Khureji Khas in North East Delhi, and Khirki

Extension and Mahatma Gandhi Park in South Delhi. From 15 January onwards, anti-CAA dharna sites were established at key locations in North East Delhi, i.e., at Seelampur, Kardampuri, Chand Bagh, Brijpuri, Noor-e-Ilahi, Khajuri Khas, Mustafabad and Jaffrabad.

The Location of Most Anti-CAA Protest Sites

The location of anti-CAA protest sites shows a distinctive pattern. Most of these sites are located in close vicinity of a local mosque. The Shaheen Bagh protest site is close to the Al-Habib Masjid. In Seelampur, the dharna site is close to the Madina Masjid. The Noorani Masjid overlooks the protest site at Khajuri Khas. At Bhajanpura the protest at Noor-e-Ilahi lay close to the Mohammadi Masjid. At Inderlok, the Badi Masjid is a few steps away from the dharna site. The Shastri Park dharna site is close to the Buland Masjid. At Bara Hindu Rao, the Masjid Jungle Wali overlooks the dharna site and at Hauz Rani, the Jameela Masjid Ahle Hadees cradles the dharna site.

It is very clear that these sites were chosen with care, with the intention of closely networking with the Muslim population of these areas and exploit fault lines.

Art as a Tool of Protest

In the backdrop of the anti-CAA protests, Delhi has seen the sudden upscaling of protest art. All over the city, protest sites were dominated by artists and poets who were performing before the protestors. The content of their art was hysterical and extremely inflammatory and amplified many times over. The amount of resources and technical expertise that were devoted to these amplified hysterical messages was enormous. One example was the techno-inflammatory assault of the poem, 'Sab Yaad Rakha Jayega' by Aamir Aziz. The content of the entire piece, the facial expressions of the performer, the music, the lights and the intensity are enough to freeze and shock any listener.[13]

The constant relay of this message to an agitated minority with policy grievances against the government had laid the base for the Delhi riots. Such messages have been constantly relayed in different forms and mediums through different persons, ranging from ghazal performances by Shubha Mudgal and performances by Prateek Kuhad to statements by Swara Bhaskar, etc.

Protest artists must also reconsider the impact that their art has had on alienating a section of the minorities, bringing the city to the edge and the subsequent eruption into violence. While such performances may be personally rewarding for them in terms of visual traction, we strongly state that Communal Violence is No Art. Playing with the lives and blood of communities to foment violence is not art, poetry and photography. Subsequent calls for peace hold no legitimacy if any kind of art has been used for alienation and subsequent communal violence.

Anti-Hindu Agitations at the CAA Protest Sites

Most of the anti-CAA protests sites in Delhi had a format that was copied extensively from the Shaheen Bagh model. Some posters and slogans were explicitly anti-CAA, anti-NRC and anti-NPR. There were posters of Babasaheb Ambedkar. Most of the posters and other media emerging from the protest sites were hinged on constitutionalism. There was a widespread display of the Indian national flag.

Some of the posters were explicitly anti-government, targeted specifically at Prime Minister Narendra Modi and Home Minister Amit Shah. Many of the posters were openly Hinduphobic and aimed at desecrating symbols that are sacred in Hinduism. There were efforts to appropriate typical symbols associated with Hindu culture as well, including visuals of bindi-sporting Hindu women wearing burkhas and the Hindu goddess Maa Kali wearing a hijab.

How Anti-CAA Protest Sites Were Violent and Undemocratic

Locals told us that protest sites across the road were a daily inconvenience. Loud slogans on loudspeakers at odd hours, sometimes beginning right from the morning or sometimes starting in the evening and continuing well into the night, caused daily disruption in the lives of residents.

Slogans with a distinctly Islamic tone were the norm, interspersed with calls for azadi. Speeches were made against the CAA, the NRC, the NPR, the government and the police and were relayed at loud decibels running into odd hours at night. Kashmir figured prominently in speeches relayed from protest sites.

Most protests and dharna sites in the area were continuously relaying these speeches from the morning onwards. Towards the evening, these protests turned frenzied. Most locals said that the occupation of metro stations and roads occurred during rush hours to cause maximum inconvenience and disruption. At night, many azadi marches were normal in the area. These would start from key points in the mohalla or the *gali* (lane) and go on till another such point. These were usually held after 10pm. Such marches heightened tensions and fear among the locals.

While locals said that the right to protest is a democratic right, it definitely did not include the right to disrupt the lives of other citizens. Since December last year, it has been claimed that the protests against the CAA, the NRC and the NPR were democratic and organic. We have been told that peaceful high-decibel protests on public-funded university

Brijpuri, North-East Delhi

campuses and public roads are democratic protests. This is a narrative that has been adopted by the Urban Naxals–Jihadis and their fronts in the national and international media, civil society, political parties and the bureaucracy. The right to the freedom of expression of every protester, ranging from the intensely Islamic, hijab-clad agitators from JMI to Sharjeel Imam from JNU, is a topic of discussion and debate in all communist and jihadi forums. However, we are compelled to ask: What are democratic protests?

Democratic protests are imbibed with the spirit of debate and discussion. In a democratic protest, the organisation leading it can be clearly identified. Such protests are conducted within the rule of law. They respect the right of persons who are not engaging in debate. Democratic protests cannot deliberately target and provoke a particular community that is largely peaceful and respects diversity. They cannot cause inconvenience to those who are not engaging in their debate. Protests in the democratic tradition cannot be based on a web of half-truths and blatant misinformation.

We found that the anti-CAA protests were neither democratic nor organic. It was observed that these protests have no single identifiable face or organisation that came across as leaders of the agitations. Thus, everyone in the protests claimed to be an independent voice, while the real planners remained in the background. The Shaheen Bagh protesters are at pains to deny any association with Sharjeel Imam, who is a major face in anti-CAA protests right since they were initiated. The anti-CAA protests have been violent, one-sided, irrational, disruptive, undemocratic and based on fear-mongering. There is not a single or even a group of leaders who represent the anti-CAA protests and who can be talked to in a democratic framework. Such protests also seem to have links with international Islamist organisations. The impeccable planning of these high-visibility protests also indicates the presence of huge foreign funds and the hand of foreign agencies.[14,15]

Evidence of the Involvement of Urban Naxal and Jihadi Organisations

Organic protests have organic formats and idioms. The Brijpuri Road right outside Arun Modern Senior Secondary School tells a story. Walls along the entire stretch are painted with

Wall graffiti at a dharna site in Mustafabad clearly showing that the protest has been imposed by the Left.

slogans. The term 'outsiders', which we constantly heard in our fact-finding process acquires a new dimension on these so-called walls of protest. The slogans on the walls on the protest site resemble a revolutionary political science format. The language seems imposed and totally out of context. The idiom seems to have been picked from some revolutionary manual discussed in a university classroom. The CAA, the NPR, the NRC, Kashmir, azadi all seem to have been foiled by themes of gender and patriarchy; the resultant cocktail seems to have been foisted on the walls of Brijpuri and all other sites that we visited. The emerging image of anxiety and psychosis defies all logic.

The debate cannot even engage critically with the issues mentioned above. We were compelled to study whether there was a pattern in these protests that were being witnessed in Delhi since at least 15 December last year.

Organisations Involved in Engineering Communal Riots in North East Delhi

The Shaheen Bagh demonstration site is a test case to understand the network that is hijacking protests by the Muslim

Wall of hate in Mustafabad.

Social media posts by organisers of Shaheen Bagh naming Pinjra Tod for engineering violence.

community, which may have grievances with government policies. In their Facebook posts, organisations like Pinjra Tod have been blamed by Shaheen Bagh organisers for constantly trying to interfere in their movement and trying to engineer violence on a mass scale. There is a large network of such organisations that have been trying to use policy contestation for engineering widespread communal disturbances.

Police Action during This Period

The period from 15 January to 20 February 2020 was the time when police action against anti-CAA protesters was at its minimum. Overall, the State was accommodative in dealing with these protests despite obvious public inconvenience at most places.

Conclusion

A careful reading makes it clear how the carefully orchestrated events mentioned above eventually culminated in the Delhi riots. The attempts to polarise the people, with possible gains in an election, were escalated to a level where their metamorphosis to a violent situation was a foregone conclusion. The dangers of the narrative spun by an Urban Naxal–Jihadi ideology, and its explicit support by mainline political parties such as the Congress and some elements of the AAP are obvious when seen in the context of the terrible loss of life, limb and property in the violence witnessed by Delhi in the final phase of this building crescendo.

The elections for the Delhi assembly were held on 8 February and the election results were announced on 11 February. Immediately thereafter, the narrative started shifting to a more aggressive and confrontational phase. The possible plan was to attract international scrutiny during the visit of the president of USA, Donald Trump, to India towards the end of February. The agitation sites were propped up in areas with a mixed population. The organisers could not have missed the possibility of violence flaring up.

From 15 February onwards, most dharnas entered a violent, aggressive phase. Waris Pathan delivered his hate speech in Gulbarga in Karnataka on 20 February.

On 23 February, a crowd of around 4,000 anti-CAA protesters entered the Malviya Nagar market. In an extremely dangerous move, azadi slogans were raised in front of the Shiva temple there. Clashes with the police occurred when the anti-CAA protesters tried to block the road. The unfolding of the events clearly points to a well-crafted strategy aimed at achieving the agenda of the hatemongers, notwithstanding its cost in lives and livelihoods.

References

1. Times News Network (TNN). 2019. 'As Video Does the Rounds, AAP MLA Denies Inciting Violence', *The Times of India*, 16 December. Available at https://timesofindia.indiatimes.com/city/delhi/as-video-does-the-rounds-aap-mla-denies-inciting-violence-in-his-speech/articleshow/72705937.cms.
2. PTI. 2020. Waris Pathan's Hate Speech: BJYM Worker Files Complaint against AIMIM Leader', *The New Indian Express*,

21 February. Available at https://www.newindianexpress.com/
nation/2020/feb/21/waris-pathans-hate-speech-bjym-worker-
files-complaint-against-aimim-leader-2106262.html.

3. HT Correspondent. 2020. '"Shaheen Bagh Protest Not a
   Coincidence, It's an Experiment": PM Modi at Delhi Election
   Rally', *Hindustan Times*, 3 February. Available at https://www.
   hindustantimes.com/assembly-elections/shaheen-bagh-protest-
   not-a-coincidence-it-s-an-experiment-pm-modi-at-delhi-election-
   rally/story-WQ6R7q5UIOTz2LSd859USI.html.

4. PTI. 2020. 'Delhi Violence Outcome of "Instigation" by
   Opposition Leaders, Including Sonia Gandhi: BJP', *The Economic
   Times*, 28 February. Available at https://economictimes.
   indiatimes.com/news/politics-and-nation/delhi-violence-
   outcome-of-instigation-by-opposition-leaders-including-sonia-
   gandhi-bjp/articleshow/74372983.cms.

5. Special Correspondent. 2019. 'Anti-CAA Protest: Rahul Gandhi
   Asks Youth and Students to Join him at Rajghat', *The Hindu*,
   23 December. Available at https://www.thehindu.com/news/
   national/anti-caa-protest-rahul-gandhi-asks-youth-and-students-
   to-join-him-at-rajghat/article30377361.ece.

6. FE Online. 2020. 'Mani Shankar Aiyar Stokes Controversy with
   "Qatil" Barb at Shaheen Bagh Anti-CAA Protests', *The Financial
   Express*, 15 January. Available at https://www.financialexpress.
   com/india-news/mani-shankar-aiyar-stokes-controversy-with-
   qatil-barb-at-shaheen-bagh-anti-caa-protests/1823558/.

7. India.com News Desk. 2020. "Attack on Students Is a Blot on
   the Nation," Says Shashi Tharoor as He Joins Anti-CAA Protests
   at Jamia & Shaheen Bagh', *India.com*. Available at https://www.
   india.com/news/india/dissent-is-precious-says-shashi-tharoor-as-
   he-joins-anti-caa-protest-at-jamia-shaheen-bagh-3907456/.

8. To watch the video, see https://timesofindia.indiatimes.com/
   topic/Bhaskare/videos/news/anti-caa-protest-govt-fuels-hatred-
   in-society-says-actress-swara-bhaskar/videoshow/73906208.
   cms?from=mdr.

9. Express News Service. 2020. 'SC Seeks Explanation from Mander
   on No Faith in SC Remark', *The New Indian Express*, 5 March.
   Available at https://www.newindianexpress.com/nation/2020/
   mar/05/sc-seeks-explanation-from-mander-on-no-faith-in-sc-
   remark-2112362.html.

10. Express News Service. 2020. 'Counsel Kids in Shaheen Bagh,
    May Suffer Mental Trauma: NCPCR', 22 January. Available

at   https://indianexpress.com/article/cities/delhi/counsel-kids-in-shaheen-bagh-may-suffer-mental-trauma-ncpcr-6228713/.

11. PTI. 2020. 'BJP Mocking Me Ever Since I Recited "Hanuman Chalisa": Kejriwal', *The Hindu*, 8 February. Available at https://www.thehindu.com/elections/delhi-assembly/bjp-mocking-me-ever-since-i-recited-hanuman-chalisa-kejriwal/article30769353.ece.

12. 'General Election to Vidhan Sabha, Trends & Results', Election Commission of India, February 2020.

13. To watch Aamir Aziz recite the poem, visit https://www.youtube.com/watch?v=PHk_5gEXDY0.

14. https://www.msn.com/en-in/news/other/delhi-riots-links-to-zakir-naik-saudi-arabia-pfi-established-in-police-probe/ar-BB16jpht

15. https://www.indiatoday.in/india/story/delhi-riots-links-to-zakir-naik-saudi-arabia-pfi-established-in-police-probe-1696849-2020-07-04

SIX

THE FINALE: RIOTS IN NORTH EAST DELHI

Introduction

The orchestrated strategy of the Urban Naxal–Jihadi elements shifted into high gear from mid-February. From 15 February onwards, the strategy at the protest sites changed. The language and the posturing became more violent and aggressive, possibly in response to the hands-off approach taken by the government and the Delhi police. The timing was possibly inspired by the high media visibility and the possibility of internationalising the issue as President Trump was scheduled to visit India in the last week of February.[1] The nature and format of the anti-CAA protests changed suddenly and an all-India, as well as a Delhi-specific pattern, emerged subsequently. This chapter describes the third and fourth phases of the Delhi riots.

Aggression Through Speeches

As was the case during the previous phases, even at this stage, hate speeches formed a very important part in escalating the general atmosphere of violence and aggression in the anti-CAA protests. On 17 February, Umar Khalid, a student leader, made a speech in Amravati in Maharashtra. In this speech, he exhorted the largely Muslim audience to come out in large numbers when the American president visited India.

I promise that when Donald Trump will visit India on 24 February, we will show how Prime Minister Narendra Modi and his government is trying to divide the country and tearing apart the principles of Mahatma Gandhi.... We will come out on streets in huge numbers to tell [the US President] that people of India are fighting to bring everyone together.[2]

Khalid then paused and asked the crowd, 'Will you come?' The answer was a resounding 'yes'. Khalid made this speech while addressing a rally in Maharashtra's Amravati on 17 February.

He also invoked the Ayodhya verdict and argued that Muslims did not revolt after the Supreme Court ruling. Inciting and misleading the mob, he further claimed that the Modi government brought the CAA to harm the Muslims. The CAA, however, doesn't apply to Indian citizens.[3]

Escalation of Anti-CAA Protests in Delhi

Two major sites of anti-CAA protests were escalated on 22–23 February. They were geographically far apart, yet the pattern in the escalation of the riots at these sites was eerily similar. One site was in South Delhi at Malviya Nagar and the other in North East Delhi.

On 23 February, a crowd of around 5,000 anti-CAA protesters from the protest site at Hauz Rani came out on the streets. They marched through the Malviya Nagar Police Station under a police escort. They raised azadi slogans on the way. In an extremely provocative move, they stood in front of the Shiva temple at Malviya Nagar and raised slogans for around 10 minutes. There were clashes with the police when they tried to block the main road there. Though they were restrained by police action, the same pattern was repeated successfully in Jaffrabad in North East Delhi.

Demography of North East Delhi

Before we deliberate on the site in North East Delhi where the Delhi riots happened, let us examine the demography of the area. As per the 2001 census data, it has the highest population growth rate amongst all districts of Delhi. Further, it has the lowest literacy rate in Delhi. It has nine villages and hence there is some constituent rural population. Finally, this district also has the lowest rates of male and female work participation amongst the districts of Delhi, i.e., there is a lot of unemployment here. As per the data of 2011 census, it ranks first in population density amongst all Delhi districts at 35,166 persons per square km. All this offers ready tinder for easy radicalisation.

There are a number of Salafi madrasas that have come up in the area. For instance, locals say that in the Bab ul Uloom Madrasa, Sharia courts are held on a regular basis. One of the main law and order issues identified through on-the-ground interviews was the presence of illegal poultry markets and illegal slaughter in many areas. For instance, as per ground reports, in Mustafabad area, 315 slaughterhouses were operating illegally. Residents have lodged their complaints with the Municipal Corporation of Delhi (MCD). However, no action was reported to have been taken.

The other issue here is the presence of illegal kabad (junk) markets, which is the mainstay of the economic operations in the neighbourhood. This is also the hub of stolen goods like mobiles and cars, where stolen cars are disassembled and sold.

The area is also prone to criminal activity, where snatchings occur all too frequently. The Mandoli Prisons Complex is a hub of drugs and crime. The North East district has nearly 1,500 declared bad characters with the Seelampur–Jaffrabad belt reportedly being crime-infested. In areas like Kabir Nagar and Sunder Nagri, police raids are frequent.

Throughout our fact-finding process, locals, both Hindus and Muslims, reported that the population profile in the region had changed due to the influx of persons from UP. The outsiders have no deep links and permanent interests in the area and these were the people who comprised the bulk of dharna protesters at anti-CAA protest sites.

Anti-CAA Dharna Sites in North East Delhi Were Not Peaceful

The details of dharna hotspots in Delhi have been given in the report submitted by the GIA to the government of India. In this section, we take a closer look at the day-to-day events in North East Delhi, with a comparison to what happened in South Delhi. After the riots, one of the main questions that we faced in the field in North East Delhi was if the dharna sites established in the area were peaceful. The other question that faced us was the nature of the action taken by the police in Delhi.

Data collected from the ground reveals that the dharna sites systematically established in Delhi since mid-December were far from peaceful. There were a total of 13 cases of rioting registered against anti-CAA protesters in the central, southern and eastern ranges of Delhi. Of these, from 16–20 December, seven cases of rioting and violence against anti-CAA protesters were registered in the eastern range itself. The riot-affected North East Delhi falls within this range. The locus of most of these rioting incidents by anti-CAA protesters was Road Number 66 (referred to by the locals as 66 Foota Road) connecting the Grant Trunk (GT) Karnal Road and Wazirabad Road. Violence in this period was concentrated between Seelampur and Jaffrabad. There were a number of hotspots on Road Number 66 which routinely saw violence. These included the Janta Colony, Kabir Nagar and Kardampuri. It is noteworthy that in all the seven incidents of violence in North East Delhi in December, the Delhi police was subject to intense stone pelting and public property was also destroyed.

Field data has shed important light on the incidents of violence in Jaffrabad on 17 and 20 December. On Tuesday, 17 December, there were clashes between the Delhi police and anti-CAA protesters on the Seelampur–Jaffrabad stretch. After tear-gassing by the police, the local leaders made several rounds of intense appeals to the crowd, which subsequently dispersed. The Delhi police then appealed to local leaders of the area to help maintain peace on 20 December, a Friday, which is an obligatory day of worship for the Muslims.

In the lead-up to that day, the police held several meetings with local leaders of all masjids in the area. After namaz on that day, a crowd of almost 40,000 persons descended on the roads of Jaffrabad, sloganeering against the CAA and making calls for azadi. The local leaders of the area again negotiated with the crowds who had by then gathered in front of the police station. The crowd remained agitated till around 2 o'clock the next morning.

The Delhi police, along with local leaders of the community such as Maulana Muhammad Daud Amini and Maulana Muhammad Shamim, consistently appealed to people from loudspeakers to disperse. However, from 17–20 December, the influence of local leaders seemed to have waned due to consistent pressure from 'outside elements in the area'. Leaders of the community were assaulted and abused in Jaffrabad.

Both these instances clearly belie the claim being made by vested interests in the national and international media that the Delhi police was anti-Muslim. Field data says that they worked with local Muslim leaders to maintain peace in the area.

It is noteworthy that around the same time that the anti-CAA protesters were violent in the central and southern police ranges, four such cases were reported in December, which re-establishes the fact that anti-CAA protests throughout the city were intermittently violent.

The period from 15 December 2019 to 25 February 2020 was the time when more dharna sites were established in various parts of Delhi. The GIA report clearly outlines the locations of these sites. In North East Delhi itself, there were seven such sites operational, where the Shaheen Bagh model was replicated: the dharna sites were established by local women and they were situated on public spaces near metro stations. Most of these sites relayed a steady stream of anti-government, anti-CAA, anti-NPR and anti-NRC rhetoric. There were slogans of azadi, in support of freedom for Kashmir, that were relayed from these sites. Some of the bigger dharna sites like Shaheen Bagh had openly anti-Hindu rhetoric. These sites often erupted into small- to medium-sized rallies in their respective localities at odd hours—in the evening and at night. For a period of eight weeks, these sites were working in tandem with organisations like AISA, Pinjra Tod and Marxist teachers and student organisations to create permanent fissures between Hindus and Muslims in the areas of their operation. They also alienated local Muslim community leaders. Apart from this, they were also a source of public inconvenience.

Table 6.1: Events in North East Delhi from 22 February 2020 Onwards

Date	Event
Saturday, 22 February 2020	Women anti-CAA protesters enter the Jaffrabad Metro Station at 5pm.
Sunday, 23 February 2020	The same women block the two carriageways on Road Number 66 at Jaffrabad at 2am.
Sunday, 23 February 2020	The road is blocked, cutting off a population of over 25 lakh from Delhi and UP.
Sunday, 23 February 2020	Around 8am, the crowd at Jaffrabad blocking the road swells to around 3,000 men and women. Locals from adjoining areas join the Jaffrabad blockage. The crowd refuses to talk to the Delhi police.
Sunday, 23 February 2020	Around 12.30pm, this crowd tries to block the Wazirabad Road. They also go towards the petrol pump at Bhajanpura (subsequently burnt on 24 February).
Sunday, 23 February 2020	Around 3.17pm, the crowd tries to march towards Seelampur T-point but is stopped.

Date	Event
Sunday, 23 February 2020	Kapil Mishra (a local BJP Leader) comes to Maujpur around 3.30pm. Locals at Maujpur assemble there and sing bhajans. They ask the Delhi police to remove the Jaffrabad blockage, after which, they say, they too will move out. Violence between two communities starts at night in Chand Bagh, where stone pelting is reported.
Monday, 24 February 2020	Led by the anti-CAA protesters at Chand Bagh, violence breaks out at Bhajanpura.
Monday, 24 February 2020	The first FIR for violence at Shiv Vihar is registered against a Muslim mob that started attacking shops and houses.

The violence that happened in the area continued till 25 February.

More illustratively, North East Delhi had been tense for almost eight weeks. On 22 February, a Saturday, at around 10.30pm, door-to-door campaigning was done in Janta Colony, to mobilise people to come on the roads for a roadblock. This is a major slum area. An anti-CAA protest site at Chand Bagh, Yamuna Vihar Road had already been set up since mid-December. The protesters had been exhibiting random disruptions and aggression since then. Moreover, since mid-January, the protesters seemed to have worked on a strategy to block main roads. These protesters moved from the metro station and blocked the main Jaffrabad Road at around 1.30am on 23 February.

The banners at Jaffrabad contained anti-CAA, anti-NPR, anti-NRC slogans. Some locals, resenting the disturbance and road blockage, also started protesting near Maujpur Chowk. It was the same site where Kapil Mishra had come at 3 pm on 23 February 2020 to address the locals.

The police was under extreme pressure as there was less than a kilometre separating the anti-CAA protestors and the agitating locals. The police had installed barricades between the two groups of protesters to avoid any untoward incident. The locals declared that they had no intention to protest but were compelled to do so after the Road Number 66 were blocked by anti-CAA protesters at the Jaffrabad Metro Station. They were of the opinion that the neighbourhood could not afford to block off of this important road. They also said that they would not allow another Shaheen Bagh to be set up in their locality.

The police, however, did not want to use force on the protesters until all options of persuasion were exhausted. Therefore, it was exploring all possibilities of negotiation. The deputy commissioner of police (DCP) Ved Prakash Surya approached two respected local leaders, Maulana Muhammad Daud Amini and Maulana Muhammad Shamim from the area, from Idgah Jaffrabad and Bab ul Uloom Madrasa respectively. Their support was enlisted in speaking to the anti-CAA protestors and getting the carriageway unblocked. Other imams of the area too had assembled at the madrasa. The police took all of them to the protest site. The place was spilling over with protesters. Using microphones provided by the cops, the imams and maulanas tried to persuade the crowd to allow the traffic to move. Surprisingly, however, none of the protesters paid any heed to their requests. This was an unusual occurrence for the maulanas, as both commanded respect in the Muslim community of the area. The elderly maulana of the Idgah was almost in tears, disheartened by the unprecedented show of disrespect, a first for him. Maulana Shamim too wondered who the women were, who did not listen to the imams from the local places of worship. Did they belong to the area?

The women continued blocking the carriageway through the night. The next day, i.e., 23 February was the day that Chandrashekhar Azad Ravan of the Bhim Army had given a call for a Bharat bandh. The same day, US President Donald Trump was on his India visit. The maulanas had returned to the protest site the same night and the next day as well, as they continued deliberations on how to help get the carriageway cleared. Road Number 66 that was blocked is strategically critical; it is the lifeline that connects GT Karnal Road to Wazirabad Road at one end and the Eastern Peripheral Expressway at the other. The anti-CAA protesters had refused to clear the road for traffic. Meanwhile, some miscreants stone-pelted the vehicle the maulanas had boarded. The driver jumped out and the maulanas too stepped out. The protesters started abusing the maulanas and imams. They called them brokers of the police and the government. The slogans being shouted also implied that the maulanas should be ashamed as they had come in a police vehicle.

The protest continued as the road remained blocked. At around 1am, a similar modus operandi of blocking the road was adopted at Chand Bagh, too. Blocking the Jaffrabad Road effectively cut off the area from a population of approximately 25 lakh from Delhi and UP from three sides, two of which were already blocked. Around 300 protesters were still on the road under the Jaffrabad Metro Station at around 6am on 23 February. Around 9am, a crowd of locals started to build up at Maujpur Chowk. They wanted the Jaffrabad blockage to be removed as it was completely cutting them off from the city centre.

They also knew from the Shaheen Bagh experience that once a dharna site was established, it had become impossible to dismantle it. It is noteworthy that both Road Number 66 and Wazirabad Road are the lifelines of North East Delhi that connect GT Karnal Road and the Eastern Peripheral Expressway, and the Signature Bridge-Loni Road Highway respectively. This led to the first round of violence between the two groups. The crowds of both the communities were almost equal in numbers as they started to collect at Maujpur and Jaffrabad respectively, separated by just 300 metres.

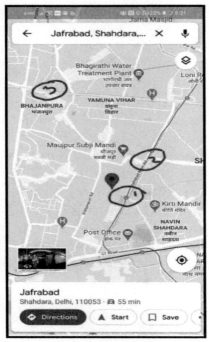

(1) The site of the road blockage by anti-CAA protesters at 1.30am on 23. February; (2) Maujpur Chowk, where local crowds mobilised on 23 February; and (3) The site of the Bhajanpura blockage and violence on 24 February.

The tension was simmering in the area as a result of which locals had started gathering on the roads. Hindus mobilised primarily due to anxieties generated by the total blockage of Jaffrabad Metro Station by the Muslim women on 23 February. Locals were very agitated by the resultant blocking of roads on three sides, GT Karnal Road, Wazirabad Road and at Chand Bagh.

There were heated verbal exchanges and confrontations between the groups at both the places, which was soon followed by stone pelting. The locals at Maujpur Chowk got caught in between stone pelting from Jaffrabad and Kabir Nagar. As the day advanced, the tension escalated and at 3.05pm, locals made calls to the police control room. Police found it difficult to protect the locals from stone pelting from two sides.

BJP leader Kapil Mishra was at the spot at 3pm, as some people had gone to call him to diffuse the situation. Since he is a locally respected person, the police sought his help to talk to the people and help clear the place. Mishra asked the police to remove the anti-CAA protesters from the Jaffrabad Metro Station.[4] This was around 4.30pm. He posted this on Twitter at 5pm on 23 February: 'We have given a three-day ultimatum to the Delhi Police to get the Jaffrabad and Chand Bagh road cleared. After this, do not try to convince us, we would not listen to you either. Three days.'

The blocking of the Jaffrabad Road on 23 February was an immediate trigger for a situation that had been simmering for almost a period of eight weeks, all across Delhi in general and in this area in particular.

This led to a fear psychosis among the locals of the area. A local, during our investigation, said, 'Madam hum doosra Shaheen Bagh apne area me nahin chahte the. Kapil Mishra toh wahan baad me aaya. Hum logon ne soch liya tha ki nahin hone denge.' (Madam, we did not want another Shaheen Bagh in our area. Kapil Mishra came to the site afterwards. We had already decided that we shall not allow that to happen here.)

Skirmishes took place between these two groups of people on the streets on 23 February, including stone pelting that, according to the police, was brought under control with tear gas. However, this control proved ephemeral. Locals said that the cops were concentrating mainly on the Jaffrabad protest site, while tensions were simmering in a larger area. By the night of 23 February, large groups of Hindus and Muslims had mobilised on the roads and the area was rife with incidents of stone pelting and skirmishes.

The next day, on 24 February, the maulanas from Jaffrabad invited some protesting women to the Bab ul Uloom Madrasa for deliberations. Eight women turned up for this discussion.

The maulanas tried to reason with them, saying that they appreciated their concerns regarding CAA, NRC and they also agreed that protesting was their democratic right. However, they added that their protests should not cause inconvenience to the general public by blocking the main road. They could sit in the service lane of the road or in the metro station parking lot, to which the women argued that their numbers were too big to fit into the parking area. Thus, discussions continued around for one hour. Finally, the women agreed to clear one side of the carriageway to let the traffic move.

While the DCP interacted with the maulanas, the station house officer (SHO) contained the local protesters at Maujpur Chowk. The Muslim religious leaders continued exhorting the anti-CAA protesters to vacate the carriageway. Meanwhile, some women started stone pelting. One stone hit the SHO of Jaffrabad, Lekhraj, whose leg injury had not healed even after 20 days. One stone was aimed at the maulana of the Bab ul Uloom Madrasa too but a boy from Gali Number 43 shielded him. The women again started abusing the maulanas. After a while, some of them went to the madrasa and kept some bangles at the gate as a symbol of protest against the maulanas for their support to the police.

The very same day, a police force was deployed in large numbers in the area. Rioting had happened in areas of Kardampuri, Chand Bagh, Khajuri Khas, Brijpuri, Ghonda, Noor-e-Ilahi, Gawndi, Kabir Nagar and Gokulpuri areas. Lives were lost in these areas of North East Delhi but Jaffrabad remained comparatively contained.

Events of 24 February

On 24 February the situation rapidly spun out of control. This day saw the petrol pump at Bhajanpura being burnt[5] and prohibitory orders under Section 144 of the Code of Criminal Procedure (CrPC)—which bans the assembly of four or more people—imposed in areas of North East Delhi. The police wanted to be extra careful since the last day's attempt to block Wazirabad Road near Chand Bagh. Under such prevailing tension, the police was very cautious on 24 February in not letting the crowd spill over to the main Bhajanpura Road from Chand Bagh. The police on the scene tried all possible ways to dispel the protesting anti-CAA crowd without resorting to force or aggression and in keeping with their general policy to explore all possibilities of negotiation and dialogue. They made announcements on mikes, asking the protestors to vacate the area, but the latter did not budge. Instead, they raised the volume of sloganeering and tried to provoke the police when they approached the protesters.

Amit Sharma, DCP Shahdara, was specially deployed at Chand Bagh, which comes under the purview of the Dayalpur Police Station in North East Delhi. The DCP was assisted by Anuj Kumar Sharma, assistant commissioner of police (ACP) of Gukulpuri, head constables Ratan Lal and Brijesh and other police personnel. The number of anti-CAA protesters had increased manifold. Wazirabad Road has Muslim-dominated colonies—Brijpuri, Chand Bagh, Mustafabad, etc.—at the back and have exits on the main road. All of a sudden, thousands of people swarmed out from those lanes. The protesters outnumbered the police party as a sea of rioters swarmed towards the main Bhajanpura Road from the lanes and by-lanes of the Muslim-dominated areas, with Muslim women in good numbers.[6]

DCP Amit Sharma and ACP Anuj Kumar, along with two other constables, tried to have a dialogue with them as they simultaneously tried to not let the road get blocked. The crowd became aggressive as their numbers swelled to 20,000–30,000. Violence then broke out almost immediately, as the protesting women attacked the police officers with stones, knives and swords hidden beneath their burkhas. One of the women pushed Amit Sharma, due to which his helmet came off, making him more vulnerable to their attacks. As his helmet fell, some other rioters repeatedly hammered his head with rods and sticks. The rioting mob was equipped with bricks, stones, rods, hockey sticks and pistols. ACP Anuj Kumar and the constables too were pelted with stones. A large stone hit the ACP's helmet, breaking it into pieces and leaving his head unprotected from the stones pelters. Meanwhile, the seriously injured DCP Amit Sharma kept pushing the crowd backwards. As the commanding officer, he instructed the police to use tear-gas shells to disperse the crowd. As this was happening, head constable Ratan Lal was shot by rioters and he fell. As per instructions from senior officers present at the scene, police personnel led him to safety towards Yamuna Vihar, another neighbourhood in the area.[7]

The police did not want to fire as a majority of the rioters were women and children. The crowd was too close to the cops, which made even tear-gassing ineffective. The police tried to contain the aggressive crowd with canes and shields but they were outnumbered by the sea of rioters. The police party was caught between the violent rioters from three sides and a high iron railing on the fourth. The unprovoked attack on the police continued brutally. Amit Sharma was repeatedly hit on his head with iron rods and hockey sticks. The killer mob appeared to be bent on lynching police officers. The DCP fell unconscious on the road. When ACP Anuj Kumar turned around from where he was caught up amidst the crowd, he realised that the commanding officer was not to be seen. He fought his way through the crowd and found him lying unconscious. He tried to rescue the unconscious DCP with help from commandos Mohit and Pradeep.[8] They lifted him towards the 6-foot-high iron railing and climbed over it. Then they had to climb over two other 5-foot-high railings. The police were surrounded by attacking rioters and the railing worked as a wall. They managed to rescue the grievously injured DCP safely to the other side of the railing. Grievous injuries were sustained by ACP Anuj Kumar while saving his senior officer. While describing the incident, the ACP said:

On February 24, Shahdara DCP Amit Sharma got injured and fell unconscious besides the divider of Wazirabad Road in Chand Bagh where people had turned violent. Two other police personnel and I got him up and took him to the Yamuna Vihar side. This was done while stones were being pelted at us by the violent mob.[9]

The murderous mob, including women, followed them with stones, sticks and rods in their hands. They kept stone pelting and attacking the police with rods. Some people from the Hindu community came to rescue police from the Muslim rioters. Heart-wrenching videos of assault on the police have surfaced on social media afterwards.[10]

DCP Amit Sharma was brought to the nearby Mohan Nursing Home for immediate medical assistance. Ratan Lal had already been brought here. After first-aid, it was decided to take both to the Guru Teg Bahadur (GTB) Hospital for further treatment. The rioters had followed the police officers to the hospital, pelting stones and vandalising and torching Mohan Nursing Home and the official car of the DCP. [11]

Amit Shama and Ratan Lal were taken to GTB Hospital in a private vehicle. In spite of the efforts of the doctors, however, Ratan Lal could not be saved. He died responding to the call of duty.[12]

Due to severe head injuries, the DCP was required to have a CT scan. As it could not be done at GTB, he was taken to Max Super Speciality Hospital at Patparganj. He had internal bleeding and went through a major neurosurgery that lasted nearly four to five hours. According to the medical reports, the left part of his head had been repeatedly attacked with sticks and iron rods, which has rendered some parts permanently damaged.

The attack on police officials left head constable Ratan Lal martyred and DCP Amit Sharma with a grievous head injury. The post-mortem report of Ratan Lal has confirmed that he was shot dead and sustained some other injuries on his body. The bullet shot penetrated through the left shoulder to the heart.

Amit Sharma is 35 years old and the father of two children—a five-and-a-half-year-old daughter Adya and a seven-month-old son Aditya. Amit's wife Pooja, a childhood friend, has seen him come out of the jaws of death. Like family members of all police officers, Pooja and her daughter are brave. She reminisces how for four days after the incident, she could barely focus on her children, as her attention was entirely taken up with worry and concern for her husband's life.

Amit needed to be hospitalised for 11 days, and it was difficult for him to sit or talk properly for several more days after that. He could not believe that a huge mob of 20,000 to 30,000 had surrounded the police officers and tried to lynch them. His biggest guilt is that he could not save Ratan Lal.[13]

Forty-two-year-old Ratan Lal is survived by his wife, Poonam Devi and three children, two daughters and a son, who study in class 7, 5 and 3 respectively. The constable with the large moustache, which he lovingly cared for, was particular about his fitness which he maintained through regular exercise. A Rajput from Rajasthan's Sikar district, Ratan Lal—the brightest among his siblings—had harboured dreams of joining the force since childhood. After his death, the police department tried to contact his family members but was unable to reach them on the phone. In the end, his photo needed to be shared on social media and TV channels. This is how his family came to know about his tragic death. It was only then that they contacted the Gokulpuri Police Station and reached the hospital.[14]

Ankit Sharma, another martyr, was 26 years old. He had graduated with honours in Hindi from DU's prestigious Hansraj College. He and his family celebrated when he was selected to be part of the Intelligence Bureau, India's internal security organisation) in 2017. He, too, had wanted to join the police force, so the job at IB was like a dream come true for him.

Everything in life was going well for Ankit, till 25 February. A promising young life was cut short and the happiness of the family turned into perennial grief.

Ankit's post-mortem report shows 51 injuries. Recently, the investigating police has arrested one Salman as one of the culprits. According to media reports, he has disclosed that he and some other Muslim boys had covered Ankit's body with a black cloth and they had pulled him to Tahir Hussain's house. This was the same house from where all the paraphernalia of rioting has been recovered. This was the same house, from whose rooftop petrol bombs were launched and the targets attacked. There were 10 to 14 men were involved in lynching and killing of Ankit Sharma. Salman himself has confessed to stabbing Ankit at least 14 times. His face was disfigured and he was thrown into the Brijpuri nullah.

News of such heart-wrenching deaths is heard from terrorism-infested countries like Syria where Islamic fundamentalists and ISIS kill people with such brutality. The modus operandi of this kind of killing that was adopted during the riots points to possible links to international organisations. The gory details of Ankit's death bring fresh memories of the brave Saurabh Kalia's gruesome murder by Pakistan forces, whose body had been mutilated in a similar manner during the Kargil War.

The incident has raised many unanswered questions. How did the Muslim rioters come to know that Ankit was an IB official? It isn't usual for a civilian to know the identity of an intelligence official in an area. Then how was it that Ankit's killers found out? Were they helped by some outside agency? Why was such an inhuman and gory way of killing chosen? Was he murdered at Tahir Hussain's house? Was Tahir himself involved in the brutal murder? Above all, has such news stopped affecting the society we live in?

It needs to be remembered that Ankit Sharma was not an individual but a representative of an institution—an institution which a section of the society loathes. His barbaric murder is an attack on the sovereignty of the state and the government representing it. His murder is an insult (or was it meant to be a message) to the country's intelligence agencies.

Why did the rioters pelt the police with stones? Why did they shoot them? Why did they lynch them? What was the fault of these police officials? They had not enacted or implemented the CAA. They had simply been performing their duty of maintaining law and order. Security forces put their lives on the line in the interest of the nation, even neglecting their families to serve the society. Then why are they always at the receiving end of such violence and aggression? They too have children, parents and families. Are they not human? Do they have no human rights? Do they deserve such brutality at the hands of very citizens whom they safeguard? The society at large needs to ponder over such disturbing questions and the safety of our security forces.

The open riots on the main highway in Bhajanpura added to the escalation of violence. On 24 February, similar violence had taken place in all the localities in North East Delhi. The rioting continued through 25 February.[15]

Conclusion

The national and international media organisations, as well as responsible organisations like the Delhi Commission for Minorities, made statements on the selected targeting of Muslim population in riot-hit areas and on the alleged inefficiency of the police.[16]

In our fact-finding mission we found that most of the riot-hit areas where street violence has happened are Muslim-dominated areas or adjoining such areas. Karawal Nagar assembly constituency is a Hindu-dominated area and also has Hindu casualties. The areas dominated by different communities are also interspersed. For example, Shiv Vihar and Karawal Nagar are Hindu-dominated areas but Shiv Vihar is a part of East Karawal Nagar which is a part of the Mustafabad assembly constituency and a Muslim-dominated area.

Table 6.2: *Area-Wise Population Percentage*

Area	Total Population	Hindus	Muslim
Jaffrabad	54,601	27.60%	70.63%
Mustafabad	127167	21.62%	78.05%
Karawal Nagar	2,24,281	88.88%	10.44%

Source: Population Census 2011.

Apart from this, in areas like Bhajanpura, there has been a major loss of property for high-value business establishments owned by Hindus. This has hit the poorest most, who used to work here to earn their living. Some of the affected families from both communities are so poor that they could not even afford the last rites of their dead.

The Delhi police, along with local community leaders like Maulana Daud and Maulana Shamim, consistently appealed to people to disperse, but it was all in vain. Weeks before the riots, back on 17–20 December, the influence of local leaders had waned due to consistent pressure from 'outside elements in the area'. Leaders of the community were assaulted and abused in Jaffrabad.

Local leaders believed that some of the women, who sat on protest on 22 February at night, might have been outsiders. The rioting has ended but it has left behind deep scars of mistrust and agony. Now, it is up to the religious leaders to play a proactive role in establishing trust between the two communities.

(This write-up is based on a number of primary field interviews conducted by the research \team of GIA. There are interviews with Maulana Mohammad Daud Amini and Maulana Mohammad Shamim, both of whom are respected community

members in Jaffrabad. We spoke to Pooja Sharma, wife of DCP Amit Sharma. We also spoke to locals in Jaffrabad from both communities who did not want to be identified. Research ethics demand that we keep their names confidential. For most of the incidents and events mentioned in this chapter, we triangulated data.)

References

1. Aslam, Saira. 2020. 'All You Need to Know about Trump's India Visit', *The Hindu*, 22 February. Available at https://www.thehindu.com/news/national/watch-donald-trump-visit-to-india/article30887793.

2. Pandya, Jay. 'Umar Khalid's Call for "Huge Numbers" during Trump's Visit Out; "Planned Plot', Says SAD', *Republicworld.com*. Available at https://www.republicworld.com/india-news/politics/akali-dals-manjinder-sirsa-alleges-delhi-riots-were-pre-planned.html.

3. Menon, Aditya. 2020. 'What Did Umar Khalid Exactly Say in His Speech in Amravati', *The Quint*, 18 March. Available at https://www.thequint.com/news/politics/umar-khalid-amit-shah-delhi-police-meenakshi-lekhi-devendra-fadnavis.

4. Express News Service. 2020. 'Kapil Sharma Gives Ultimatum to Delhi Cops, Says Clear Roads in Three Days Or We Will Take to Streets', *The Indian Express*, 24 February. Available at https://indianexpress.com/article/cities/delhi/clear-roads-in-3-days-or-we-will-take-to-streets-bjp-leader-kapil-mishra-6283176/.

5. Gothi, C. 2020. 'Rioters Set Petrol Pump on Fire in Northeast Delhi's Bhajanpura', *India Today*, 24 February. Available at https://www.indiatoday.in/india/story/bhajanpura-petrol-pump-fire-1649533-2020-02-24.

6. Zee Media Bureau. 2020. 'Burqa-Clad Women Who Attacked Delhi Police Identified', *Zee News India*, 13 March. Available at https://zeenews.india.com/delhi/breaking-news-delhi-riots-burqa-clad-women-who-attacked-delhi-police-identified-2269388.html.

7. Based on field interviews by the GIA fact-finding team.

8. These details were gleaned based on the interview with the DCP's wife.

9. Asian News International (ANI). 'ACP Anuj Sharma Narrates Tale of Rescuing His Senior during Delhi Violence', 5 March. Available at https://www.aninews.in/news/national/general-news/acp-anuj-sharma-narrates-tale-of-rescuing-his-senior-during-delhi-violence20200305124618/.

10. To watch the video, see https://timesofindia.indiatimes.com/videos/city/delhi/delhi-riots-video-of-day-2-violence-shows-mob-attacking-cops/videoshow/74490792.cms;   and   https://www.youtube.com/watch?v=ANvGq63j0Hc.

11. To watch the video, see https://news.abplive.com/videos/news/india-delhi-clashes-know-what-happened-inside-the-premises-of-mohan-nursing-home-1167592.

12. Pandey, M.C. 2020. 'Delhi Violence: Police Pay Tribute to Slain Officer Ratan Lal', *India Today*, 25 February. Available at https://www.indiatoday.in/india/story/delhi-violence-ratan-lal-head-constable-tribute-1649926-2020-02-25.

13. Based on field interviews by the GIA fact-finding team.

14. TNN. 2020. 'Head Constable Ratan Lal Who Always Took Up Tough Challenges', *The Times of India*, 25 February. Available at https://timesofindia.indiatimes.com/city/delhi/cop-who-always-took-up-tough-challenges/articleshow/74291710.cms.

15. ET Online. 2020. 'Delhi Communal Riots Timeline: A Blow-by-Blow Account of Three Fatal February Days', *The Economic Times*, 27 February. Available at https://economictimes.indiatimes.com/news/politics-and-nation/delhi-communal-riots-timeline-a-blow-by-blow-account-of-three-fatal-february-days/articleshow/74330917.cms.

16. Ghosh, S. 2020. 'Delhi Violence "One-Sided, Well- Planned", Says Minoritie Panel', *The Hindu*, 4 March. Available at https://www.thehindu.com/news/cities/Delhi/delhi-violence-one-sided-well-planned-says-minorities-panel/article30979785.ece.

SEVEN

CONCLUSION

Introduction

The brief timeline of events and data analysis leads to the following conclusions. First, the entire characterisation of the anti-CAA protests as peaceful is flawed. The anti-CAA protests were violent from the beginning. This is borne out by the number of cases of stone pelting and loss to public property registered against the protesters across districts of Delhi. Second, before and after the Delhi riots in North East Delhi, the Delhi police has not been anti-Muslim as alleged. Rather, the officers have worked with local Muslim community leaders and the general population to maintain peace in highly adverse circumstances and in the face of grave provocation. Third, violence against the Delhi police and locals in North East Delhi originated in the protest site at Chand Bagh. On 24–25 February, the police faced violent mobs at Jaffrabad where locals indulged in attacking them. It was here that a man named Mohammad Shahrukh fired several rounds from his weapon. Visuals of him taking on unarmed police personnel are the most revealing images of the riots. While the violence spread to other areas, the main site of provocation, Jaffrabad, remained unaffected by communal violence. Subsequently, it spread to Brijpuri, Noor-e-Ilahi and other areas which had anti-CAA protest sites. Finally, in key areas in North East Delhi like Shiv Vihar, which saw horrendous violence, the first attack was made by Muslim mobs.

Main Conclusions

1. **Riots in North East Delhi were a planned conspiracy:** The Delhi riots were pre-planned. There is evidence of an Urban Naxal–Jihadi model of revolution that has been executed in Delhi and is sought to be replicated at other places.

2. **Systematic planned radicalisation of minorities:** The riots are not genocide or a pogrom targeted at any community. They are a tragic outcome of a planned and systematic radicalisation of the minorities by an Urban Naxal–Jihadi network operating in universities in Delhi. Both Hindu and Muslim communities have suffered greatly as a consequence. The presence of jihadi organisations like PFI at dharna sites has been observed.

3. **Anti-CAA dharna sites were located and planned for the radicalisation of Muslims over a long period which ultimately led to the riots:** Around 15 December 2019 and two weeks after that, protest sites were established in all major areas that had a high concentration of Muslims. Most of these dharna sites were located close to a local masjid.

4. **Riots originated in anti-CAA protest sites:** Women sitting on dharna since 15 December 2019 came on roads, blocked metro stations and thereafter, stone-pelting mobs led to riots. (This also happened in areas as far as Malviya Nagar.) After blocking the roads, the protesters got into a confrontation with the police. The situation turned violent and communal in such areas. Rioting continued in the area from 23 to 25 February.

5. **Women used as a shield at all protest sites:** At all dharna sites, women were kept at the forefront and men operated from behind this shield. This is true of all anti-CAA dharna sites and was initially majorly experimented in Shaheen Bagh.

6. **Anxiety and fear among the locals:** Most protest sites relayed a constant stream of high-decibel sloganeering continuously for the eight weeks leading up to the riots, leading to anxiety and fear amongst the local population.

7. **Protest marches on streets, roads, markets, etc., at odd times led to chaos:** Most of the protest sites are in public spaces, under metro stations and in public parks. Anti-CAA protesters moved into key market areas, roads, metro stations at night or early mornings repeatedly, causing chaos amid the local population.

8. **The Shaheen Bagh Model:** The content of most of these protests was a mixture of Urban Naxal–Jihadi and anti-CAA, anti-NRC and anti-NPR activism. The sloganeering had anti-Amit Shah, anti-Modi and anti-fascist rhetoric. Most of these sites still have 'revolution' slogans painted on the walls. Songs from the Italian folk tradition like 'Bella Ciao' were sung daily. This was the Shaheen Bagh Model.

9. **Anti-Hindu, anti-India, anti-police and anti-government nature of the protests:** It is observed that the slogans and posters at Shaheen Bagh had a deliberately provocative, anti-Hindu content. Icons holy in Hindu culture like the Swastik and Aum were depicted in a derogatory manner. Images of the Hindu goddess Kali and bindi-sporting women were shown in burkhas. While on the one hand Islamic slogans were raised repeatedly, locals also reported 'Pakistan Zindabad' slogans. All this was being done against a backdrop of the Constitution and the Indian national flag.

10. **Jihadi mobs indulged in targeted killings, and looting and vandalising shops:** On 24 February, violence spread to Bhajanpura, Shiv Vihar, Gokulpuri, Brijpuri, Brahmpuri and the surrounding areas. There was widespread evidence of mobs of violent women and men attacking the police,

important public sites like petrol pumps and high-value properties belonging to Hindus.

11. **Riot weapons were stockpiled over a period of time:** There is evidence that high-rise buildings in the area, i.e., the house of former AAP councillor, Tahir Hussain in Khajuri Khas and the Rajdhani Public School owned by Faisal Farroque were used as depots for storing weapons like acid pouches, petrol bombs, etc. Huge catapults of the kind found in Syria were already installed on the rooftop of these buildings. This points towards elaborate preparation for riots.

12. **High-rise buildings used to launch attacks:** Once the violence started, these high-rises were used as sites for launching petrol bombs and Molotov cocktails. These buildings became vantage points for groups of rioters. Several people were killed by gunshot wounds during the 24 February violence, and there is evidence that they were victims of sniper-style sharpshooters, i.e., trained shooters firing from the rooftop of Rajdhani Public School.

13. **Links across the border:** The ISIS-style brutal killings point towards links across the border. IB official Ankit Sharma's post-mortem indicates that he was stabbed over 51 times before and after his death. It has been reported that Dilber Negi, a 23-year-old worker in a Shiv Vihar sweet shop, had his hands amputated, after which he was burnt alive.

14. **Exemplary role of local Hindu and Muslim community leaders:** The Delhi police and Hindu and Muslim community leaders worked together to contain this extremely dangerous situation. While outsiders instigated violence, local community leaders worked on the ground to establish peace. We met a number of such persons.

15. **Violence against women:** Women reported that they were harassed and faced extreme danger during the riots. We met principals from Yamuna Vihar schools who reported that the female students in their care were in a very insecure

position. It was impossible in the circumstances to hand them over to their parents and caregivers. Young schoolgirls were stranded in school campuses for a long time. The rioters took advantage of this situation and molested them on their way back home when they finally left the campus. It is alleged that the underclothes of a young woman were recovered from the house of Tahir Hussain. The dead body of a woman was allegedly recovered from the nullah at Khajuri Khas.

16. **Scheduled Caste victims:** There are a large number of victims belonging to the Scheduled Caste community and some who belonged to the weaker economic sections of society. Throughout our field survey, we saw and met victims who were daily-wagers or earned very little. Most of them live in *galis* with bare minimum sanitation and conveniences. The victims are mostly innocent bystanders. Most of them had come out of their homes for basic needs like getting milk, food, medicines, etc. They were caught unawares in the violence.

17. **Identity of the rioters:** Who were the rioters? While this is a question that will be answered by the agencies investigating the riot through CCTV and other footage, there seem to be some common features as stated by the people we met.

18. **The outsiders:** In every *gali* and road we covered, people said that the rioters were outsiders and not residents of their mohalla. The question remains as to who these outsiders were. In North East Delhi, some *galis* open out into what is technically UP. There is no sealed border. Apart from this, *baharwale* or outsiders could mean someone from the next *gali* or mohalla. For example, in Khajuri Khas we were told that outsiders came from Mustafabad. In Bhajanpura we were told that outsiders came from Chand Bagh. The crowds of rioters were very well prepared to conceal their identities. Many were wearing helmets and had blackened their faces.

19. **Outsiders from various universities in Delhi:** The outside influence is most palpable when one visits the sites of anti-CAA protests that have now been removed. They point at the involvement of a revolutionary network that engineered and managed the riot situation. Specifically, the role of organisations like Pinjra Tod in instigating violence has been mentioned by organisers of Shaheen Bagh in their social media posts. Locals in areas as far as Chand Bagh and Malviya Nagar have reported the presence of women students from JNU who were constantly instigating crowds in these areas over a period of several weeks before 23 February. We observed everywhere that the police and law enforcement agencies were on the back foot due to the large number of rioters who were also armed. The anti-CAA protestors from by-lanes and alleyways spilt out on to the streets, accompanied by armed jihadi mobs that targeted the Delhi police and civilians alike. As a result, the life of common citizens was endangered and they had to resort to self-defence in the face of rioting mobs. Those who have incurred injuries are common people who were engaged in their everyday professions. They had to form lines of defence to safeguard life and property.

20. **The violent nature of anti-CAA protests:** Anti-CAA protests have been violent from the start. Multiple incidents of violence have been reported at police stations in the North East district itself from December 2019, which preceded the incidents of 23–25 February.

Recommendations

1. **An enquiry by the NIA into the Delhi riots:** We strongly recommend that given the intensity of the violence, the investigation into the riots should be handed over to the NIA. All incidents in Delhi from 15 December 2019 should be investigated.

2. **Foreign funds and support for the violence in Delhi should be investigated by the NIA:** The planning and execution of the Delhi riots from dharna to danga indicates the involvement of foreign agencies and funds. This should be investigated by the NIA.

3. **Rehabilitation for all victims:** In light of the extreme violence suffered by the most marginal sections of society in North East Delhi, we suggest that rehabilitation work should be done expeditiously.

4. **The central government should initiate confidence-building measures:** We suggest that the central government initiate confidence-building measures amongst both communities utilising the goodwill of prominent community members. There is still simmering anger and dangerous perceptions on the ground that need to be calmed.

5. **Forensic audit of high-rise buildings:** We strongly recommend that a forensic audit of all high-rises in North East Delhi be carried out by investigating agencies.

6. **An enquiry by the NIA into the 'outsider' network:** We strongly recommend that intelligence and government agencies should investigate the 'outsider' network responsible for engineering riots in Delhi through an NIA enquiry. We recommend that the role of students, teachers, artists and organisations responsible for instilling hate through protest marches, social media posts, provocative speeches, etc., should be investigated.

7. **Direction to university authorities not to allow their campuses to be used for hate speeches and political gatherings:** We request university administrators, i.e. vice chancellors of DU, JMI, JNU and all other universities to take an audit of the use of their campuses to engineer wider disturbances in the city in the eight weeks leading up to the riots.

8. **Investigations into the funding of Shaheen Bagh-type protests:** Boarding, lodging, food, hoardings, banners,

publicity material, etc., that were used at dharna sites must have been purchased from the market. The source of funds for the same must be investigated.

9. **Legal and medical camps should be organised:** Legal and medical facilities and psychological counselling of victims including children should be arranged.

10. **The sanctity of public spaces to be maintained by all law enforcing agencies:** The police should ensure that roads, streets, parks, etc., should not be used for protests. Such gatherings should only be allowed at designated spaces.

Many unanswered questions still need to be investigated and examined in detail. The Shaheen Bagh Model was sought to be replicated not only in North East Delhi but also in key areas in South Delhi. Anti-CAA protesters were clearly following a pattern, wherein the blocking of important roads was a key strategy to isolate and immobilise large parts of the local population. The fact that the time and format of the disturbances at Malviya Nagar on 23 February were eerily along similar lines as the events that were unfolding in North East Delhi raise serious concerns for internal security.

EIGHT

GROUND STORIES AND NARRATIVES OF PAIN

Introduction

This chapter is based on the fact-finding report that was submitted to the government of India by the GIA. It gives detailed verbatim accounts of the victims of the 2020 Delhi riots and offers a close look at the horror that was unleashed on Delhi from 23 to 25 February.

The areas in North East Delhi we visited are:

1. Khajuri Khas
2. Bhajanpura
3. Chand Bagh
4. Karawal Nagar
5. Mustafabad
6. Shiv Vihar
7. Brijpuri

The local persons we met were:

1. Mohammad Istar, owner of a unisex salon
2. Ashok Kumar, owner of Ashok Foam
3. Satpal Singh, owner of Classic Paint and Sanitary Store
4. Dilip Bhandari and Shiv Kumar Raghav, owners of a motorcycle service centre
5. The family of Dinesh Kumar Khatik
6. The family of Vinod Kumar Kashyap

7. The family of Rahul Solanki
8. The family of Rahul Singh
9. Muhammad Haider Naqvi, president of the Yamuna Vihar Kindergarten Education Society, Bhajanpura.
10. The Garg family
11. Nazni Parveen, local resident
12. Pankaj Sharma, owner of D.R.P. Convent Public School
13. Bhishma Sharma, owner of Arun Modern Senior Secondary School
14. Vinod Joshi, owner of JTC Technical Education Centre
15. Puspendra Gaur, owner of an English-speaking centre
16. Wakeel Siraj, resident of Yamuna Vihar
17. Sushil, owner of a computer centre
18. Farooq Ali, resident of Ghonda
19. Navneet Gupta, owner of Horizon Institute
20. Zulfikar, resident of Maunpuri
21. Sethi, owner of Sethi Enterprises
22. Sanyog Chauhan, resident of Bhajanpura
23. Abdul Rashid aka Haji Baba, vice president, Residents' Welfare Association (RWA) and president, Minara Masjid
24. Zakeel Ahmad, resident of Yamuna Vihar <list ends>

These were the damaged schools and educational institutions that we visited:

1. D.R.P. Convent Public School, Babu Nagar, Shiv Vihar
2. Arun Modern Senior Secondary School, Brijpuri
3. JMT Technical Institute, Bhajanpura
4. Horizon Institute, Bhajanpura
5. Fahan International School, Bhajanpura
6. Rajdhani Public School, Babu Nagar, Shiv Vihar

A Ground Report from Major Sites of the Visit

Chand Bagh

Our first stop was at Chand Bagh, which derives its name from the Chand Baba Mazar situated on the road. A site revered in the area by Hindus and Muslims alike is a dargah. There are signs of damage in this site of composite faith. A few metres down, the Shri Durga Fakiri Mandir lies stoned and vandalised and closed for worship.

The Chand Baba Mazar.

From here we walked down the 4 km stretch that shows evidence of the destruction caused by the riots. A few metres down from the Chand Baba Mazar, we passed shops that had been completely burnt down and vandalised.

Vandalised and burnt shops.

We met Ashok Kumar, proprietor of Ashok Foam, which is situated in E-5 Khajuri Khas. His shop has been completely burnt down and he says the loss of property is in the range of Rs15–20 lakh. At the same place, we met Satpal Singh, owner of the Classic Paint and Sanitary Store. He estimates his loss at Rs80 lakh. With a daughter to be married soon, Satpal Singh is a broken man. We also met Dilip Bhandari, the owner

The burnt Bhandari Services shop.

The 'can' used to carry petrol.   *Ashok Foam, Khajuri Khas.*

of Bhandari Services, a service centre located at E-5 Khajuri Khas. This has also been completely burnt down. His loss can clearly be seen from the burnt site. A few goons holding rods and a can full of petrol entered his shop. They first looted the cash and then threatened everyone to vacate the shop as they wanted to set it on fire.

Tahir Hussain's house, Khajuri Khas.

A few metres from here stands the house of Tahir Hussain, the AAP councillor from this area. It is an under-construction building spread over 1,000 square yards. The media and Delhi police have taken cognisance of his involvement in the death and destruction that happened in this area. Right next door to this is the completely burnt house of former area councillor from BJP, Mahak Singh.

We went to Ankit Sharma's house, the trainee IB official who was allegedly dragged into Tahir Hussian's house and brutally executed in an ISIS-style killing. His post-mortem report clearly indicated sustained and severe torture of the kind faced by our security forces on the Indo-Pak international border. We saw the nullah from where his body, along with those of three other boys, was fished out.

The burnt house of former area councillor, Mahak Singh.

Vaishno Bhojanalaya, Shiv Vihar.

When we visited his house, Ankit's family was in Muzaffarpur for his last rites. However, the picture of the man that emerges from speaking to residents living in the locality is that of a diligent, law-abiding citizen. A helpful local, he lost his life because he went to look into the shrieks of distress that he heard. A student of Hansraj College, DU from 2010 to 2013, Ankit had worked hard to crack his entry into the IB. His family was also looking forward to getting him married.

We walked down the entire 4 km stretch witnessing burnt shops and establishments. Vaishno Bhojanalaya was totally burnt whereas other nearby shops had opened. The Siddiqui Medical Shop was open, as were other medical shops in the area.

Shops nearby Vaishno Bhojanalaya.

Vinod Kumar Kashyap: A Scheduled Caste Man Was Lynched by a Mob Shouting 'Allah-hu-Akbar'

Vinod Kumar Kashyap was lynched in Brahmpuri Street Number 1 by a mob. His son Monu survived the encounter with the mob.

Family members fondly remember Vinod as a popular community figure in the Brahmpuri area of North East Delhi. A disc jockey (DJ) by profession, he had come up the hard way. He started by dabbling in electrical work and slowly built himself up, building a house and stabilising his family. He was a Shiva bhakt (devotee) and even travelled as a Kanwariya during the annual Kanwar Yatra, held in the Hindu month of Sawan (roughly around the monsoon season). The pilgrimage is extremely tough and young men from all over the land travel to Gangotri and other places along the route of the Ganga to collect its waters, which they bear in vessels or kanwars on their shoulders. They then make the trek back to their villages, to offer this holy water to the Shiva temples. Vinod Kumar Kashyap was a well-known face in this yatra. Possessed of a strong build and imposing personality, he was lovingly called Bhola Baba or Shiv Baba by his family and friends.

On the night of 24 February, around 10.30pm, Vinod and his son Monu stepped out of the house to buy medicines for Vinod's grandson. The chemist, Kalyan Medical Store, is barely a few metres away from their house. Though the area had been tense, there was no inkling of the lynching that was to follow.

A stone hit Monu Kashyap, and the bike on which the father and son were riding slipped. As though out of nowhere, a crowd of 200 people carrying stones and shouting 'Allah-hu- Akbar' surrounded the two of them. They were attacked repeatedly till Monu pretended to be dead and lost consciousness. Social

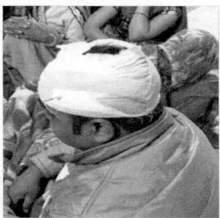

The injured Vinod Kumar Kashyap's
son Monu with 40 stitches.

Vinod Kashyap lying dead
on the roads of Brahmpuri

media videos show a dead Vinod being dragged on the streets. Bhole Baba had been lynched to death.

As he recounts this incident, Monu's bloodshot eyes are filled with tears. He has sustained at least 40 stitches on his head. Social media images show him bleeding from his head, trying to shake and slap his dead father into consciousness.

We were left with questions raging in our minds. Why should a person who stepped out to buy medicines be lynched to death? We spoke at great length to locals in the area.

We went around the area and saw the road where the incident happened. We were told that Vinod made the mistake of crossing the 'border' that exists between Hindu and Muslim areas on Wazirabad Road. As soon as someone from the other side came within grabbing distance he was caught, surrounded and lynched to death.

Dinesh Kumar Khatik: A Scheduled Caste Man Shot by a Trained Shooter

We also met the family of Dinesh Kumar Khatik, resident of House Number 326, Gali Number 5, Prem Nagar, Karawal Nagar. The 35-year-old belonged to the Scheduled Caste and lived in a joint family in a small house in the area.

Family of Dinesh Khatik

Dinesh Khatik   *Mother of Dinesh Khatik*

On 24 February, he stepped out of his house to buy some food for his children, two sons aged six and one-and-a-half. On finding shops around the house closed, he went a little further to Shiv Nagar Puliya.

According to residents and his family, he was shot from the roof of Rajdhani Public School at Shiv Vihar Puliya. He was shot from a distance of at least 200 metres with a bullet to the forehead. His family says that this can only be the work of a sniper or sharpshooter. We spoke to his brother, Suresh Kumar Khatik, who gave us a gory account of the incident. He also spoke of three to four persons who were similarly shot dead.

Dinesh owned a small inverter shop in Durgapuri. 'Madamji hame toh roz kuan khodna hai, aur roz paani peena hai.' (Madam, we have a hand-to-mouth existence and have to earn our bread daily) Life is a daily grind for this family. As we spoke to his brother, Dinesh's father sat around, shocked and maddened with grief. We met his wife Kusumlata as well, who broke down innumerable times. An uneducated woman with a child feeding at her breast, she has no hopes for the future. The small irregular income that her husband brought in has stopped. Her elder son is currently in lower kindergarten in a small neighbourhood school. She has an eye problem and cannot see properly. For her, the future is dark.

Suresh Kumar Khatik spoke of the larger-than-life fear that still exists in the locality. When we met the locals they told us that men are still out on night vigils and are alert for the smallest disturbance in the area.

Maroof Ali: He Was Shot Dead Just 50 Metres from His House

On the night of 25 February, Ghonda was tense due to news of unrest in Bhajanpura and surrounding areas. Men were awake at night for a vigil. Maroof Ali, 34, stepped out and ventured barely 50 metres from his house towards T-point in the lane in front of his house, along with five friends.

All five sustained bullet injuries. Maroof Ali, a daily-wager doing electrical repairs to earn his livelihood, was shot below his right eye and died. He leaves behind parents, brothers, a wife and two children—ten-year-old Zeenat and six-year-old Farhan.

His father Farooq says, 'We have lived here for 47 years. We have never seen such conditions in this area.' A short,

Maroof Ali's children and father.

The place where Maroof was shot dead.

dark and stoic man with a soft voice, he sees no future for Maroof's family. Nobody from the government has visited them.

Zulfikar, Siraj's Son Shot in the Mouth: Caught in the Wrong Place at the Wrong Time

Zulfikar, a daily-wager, stays in Maunpuri. On 25 February, he was returning from Jama Masjid, Ghonda after namaz when he a bullet hit him on the mouth, where it is still embedded. When we met him, his operation was imminent. He refused to be photographed.

Rahul Solanki Dead from a Bullet to the Neck: He Had Gone out to Buy Milk

After negotiating through several small galis, we finally reached Rahul Solanki's small house in Babu Nagar, Shiv Vihar. His brother, Rohit, and other male members of the family were sitting outside. Overflowing open drains and slush on the roads is evidence of the fact that these are underprivileged colonies.

Rahul Solanki's mother and brother.

The women were indoors, including his sister and mother, who lay senseless. She calls out to her dead son, moans and screams for him. She calls out to God to take her away too.

Rahul was popular in his area for being a community-driven youngster. All of 26 years, he was a trained engineer who was pursuing his master's in business administration (MBA) from a private institute in Ghaziabad. He used his skills and social network to get the roads in his locality built and repaired.

On 24 February, he had stepped out briefly with his friends to buy milk for the family. Rahul had barely exited the lane of his locality when he and his friends were confronted with a mob. His friends managed to escape but he wasn't as lucky. He caught a bullet in the neck, below his right shoulder, according to his father Hari Singh Solanki.

Nazni, neighbour of Rahul Solanki

Such was the fear in the locality that Rahul had to be cremated under the protection of paramilitary forces.

Nobody in the area knows who comprised the mob that shot Rahul. Residents of the area say that they have lived as a composite community for decades. We also spoke to Nazni Parveen, who owns a small provisions shop right outside Rahul's house. Shaheen Bagh has a larger-than-life attraction for Muslim women. She and a group of women around her spoke of the struggles of the women of Shaheen Bagh. On being asked what was it about the CAA that called for protests in that neighbourhood, they are unsure about the Act itself. 'Aapko pata hoga madam. Sarkar ko pata hoga vo aisa kyun kar rahee hai.' (You would know Madam. And the government would know why it is doing this.)

Clearly, even in a composite community that lives together, there is a divide over the CAA and Shaheen Bagh. And along with this, fear prevails in the small, dirty lanes of Shiv Vihar. This is a divide that has been assiduously created over a period of a few months. Communities that have been living together are now counting their dead.

Rahul Singh Shot in the Stomach: The Son of a Jawan Was Not Spared

Rahul Singh, who resided in Brijpuri, was a 23-year-old boy who had just finished writing his Service Selection Board (SSB) exams, Rahul was awaiting results and hoped to be selected for a government job. He was a young man looking forward to a bright future. We met his elder brother, Abhishek Singh in the small 5-foot-by-8-foot room. His father sat alongside, empty-eyed and his mother lay upstairs in a small room, sedated and senseless.

Rahul had stepped out of the house in response to calls of 'Aaa gaye, aaa gaye.' (They've come, they've come). Residents we spoke to told us that fear was palpable in the region for the previous three days. Abhishek tells us that Rahul must

Spot where Rahul Singh was shot dead

Rahul Singh's brother

have walked barely a few metres outside his house into the main Brijpuri road before he was shot dead in the stomach. Who shot him? Locals told us that the bullet came from the showroom of one Aziz Qureshi.

Rahul's father is a retired Railway Protection Force (RPF) jawan. His mother is a housewife. The family runs a small store dealing in puja material. His brother sits in a corner, dazed, unable to come to terms with the loss of his child. His voice trails off midway and he swoons in pain. Life will never be the same again for Rahul's family.

At Shiv Vihar: A Tale of Two Schools

D.R.P. Convent Secondary School in Shiv Vihar was totally burnt and destroyed on 24 February. When we spoke to the school's owners Pankaj Sharma and his wife, Meena, they narrated a heart-breaking story of destruction and damage. A majority of the students here were from around the area itself, and this temple of education was burnt down by a mob.

Burnt DRP School, Shiv Vihar

Rajdhani School rooftop used by rioters to target thearea

Temple Targeted from Rajdhani School

Destruction that happened near Rajdhani School

Immediately next door is the Rajdhani Public School, which is the highest building in the area and has been extensively covered by the media as the site from which projectiles, stones and petrol bombs were launched on people below. It is from here that many deaths occurred due to bullets fired by snipers and sharpshooters.

Structures close by, like the Hanuman mandir and the parking below, were targeted by flaming projectiles from the roof of Rajdhani Public School. The school belongs to the Fazal Education Society.

Bhajanpura as Witnessed by the Team

We spent some time on the main highway at Bhajanpura, which was the epicentre of mob violence on 24 February. This is the place where a petrol pump was looted and burnt. This is also the place where the following educational institutions were targeted by the rioting mob:

Burnt house and car near petrol pump

1. JMT Technical Institute that provides skill- and job-oriented courses to students. We met Vinod Joshi, the owner of the institute. He told us that on 24 February when his institute was attacked and burnt, there were around 40 students inside. These students had to be rescued through the back gate after breaking it open.

2. Horizon Institute: It offers medical and engineering entrance training to students. We spoke to the head of the institute, Navneet Gupta, who informed us that at the time of the mob attack, around 70 students were present inside the campus. These students were rescued from the back lanes after great difficulty.

The Garg Family: They Dropped Their Children down from the Rooftop to Escape Their Burning House

At Bhajanpura, we met the Garg family. We spoke to Preeti Garg, the feisty mother of Sanyam and Vihan, who recalled the horror of 24 February. She was cooking lunch, her mother-in-law was sitting in the house, one son was taking bath and one

Preeti Garg and her children

was sleeping when a mob approached their house and set it on fire. As the house started filling up with toxic fumes, she rushed to the roof with her children. The back lanes of her house were full of fleeing colony residents. She prayed to them for help. Residents below asked her to drop the children as they waited to catch them. She flung her sons one by one as the crowd below caught the boys. A long time after securing the children, Preeti and her mother-in-law escaped. They climbed down with the help of a makeshift ladder arranged by the neighbours. As she spoke to us her voice trembled, her eyes filled up and she cried incessantly. When we met her, the children were being treated at Madhukar Rainbow Children's Hospital, Malviya Nagar for post-traumatic stress disorder. They are unable to sleep, wake up constantly at night and are scared that 'wo phir se aa jayenge' (they'll come back).

Sanyog Chauhan: He Has a Bullet Embedded in His Back

When we met him, Sanyog Chauhan recounted the several incidents that occurred in Bhajanpura and how it flared up. He recounted how he and other shopkeepers from the area had to put up a basic defence of their shops. They kept the rioters from entering the Bhajanpura market area where the loss would have been unimaginable had the shops and people there been attacked.

During one of these vigils, a bullet grazed his chin; hit the iron bar behind him and rebounded into the back of his shoulder, where it still lies embedded. He has been advised to let it remain as the procedure to remove the bullet will be a high-risk operation.

Sanyog Chauhan,
resident of Bhajanpura.

What Happened at Bhajanpura: Rioting from Chand Bagh

We met residents of Bhajanpura who recounted the events of 24 February. Locals report that tensions in the locality started on the 23rd when the anti-CAA protest site at Chanderpuri, Chand Bagh was vacated by the police. The protesters regrouped the next day on Wazirabad Road and started to re-occupy the protest site. A small police contingent asked them to move away. This is when the mob emerged from the lanes of Chand Bagh and joined those at the anti-CAA site. They attacked the police, who were clearly outnumbered and suffered grievous injuries. As mentioned in greater detail in Chapter 7, Constable Ratan Lal was hit with stones and shot, ACP Anuj Kumar Sharma was injured and so was DCP Amit Sharma. As all three of them were taken across the road to Mohan Nursing Home, the mob too crossed the road and attacked the large petrol pump located there.

The Muslim-majority area across the road where the petrol pump was burnt in Bhajanpura.

The burnt petrol pump of Bhajanpura.

The petrol pump was looted and burnt. A liquor shop was then attacked, after which that too was looted and burnt. Locals told us that the liquor was used to make inflammable bottle bombs. It was here that educational institutions that we mentioned above were attacked and burnt by the mob.

The locals of the area cooperated with the injured policemen, taking them for first-aid to Mohan Nursing Home. They reported that within a few minutes of this, rioters followed them into the hospital, attacking the staff and damaging the building.

According to the locals, tension had been palpable in the locality since the morning. After the police had been attacked, there was complete chaos on the roads. Locals networked and had to form teams to rescue trapped residents and children.

Locals also played a role in saving the Bhajanpura market from being burnt down and looted by rioters. They rapidly downed shutters and did not allow the mob to proceed inside the market. They faced stones and bullets. Locals showed us injuries sustained due to stone pelting and firing of bullets. They, however, continued to defend life and property.

School Burnt, 22,000 Books Burnt: Arun Modern Senior Secondary School

Located on a main road sprawling over an area of 2,200 square yards, the Arun Modern Senior Secondary School was a large temple of education, with 150 computers, two projectors and a library containing 22,000 books for children. It was even equipped with smart classrooms. The management was

Vandalised and burnt, Arun Modern Senior Secondary School.

known to support many students from weaker socio-economic backgrounds with freeships and bursaries.

Today, the school lies totally burnt and destroyed. When we visited it three days post the riots, smoke was still rising from the pile of books that were burnt. The owner of the school and its employees can do little but look on stoically as the future of several children lies burnt.

Fahan International School: Another School Targeted

Fahan International School, which is situated in B3 Yamuna Vihar was also attacked on 25 February. The well-equipped school includes classrooms furnished with comfortable furniture and also provides educational toys, motivational charts and pictures from around the world, games and outdoor play equipment for the students.

Like other schools, this institution was also targeted by a mob of 150 to 200 between 1.30pm and 2pm. This whole incident was clearly recorded on CCTV cameras, which were destroyed shortly afterwards, along with the digital video recorder.

Muhammad Haider Naqvi, president, Yamuna Vihar Kindergarten Education Society.

We met Muhammad Haider Naqvi, who is the vice president of Yamuna Vihar Kindergarten Education Society, who narrated the horror he witnessed in the Fahan International School. He approached BJP leader Pramod Gupta, the councillor of the B3 Yamuna Vihar area to seek some help. Mr Gupta not only assured him but also protected the school.

Experiencing the Terror: Locals Struggle to Protect Themselves

We met Mohammad Istar, who runs a unisex salon in the C3 Yamuna Vihar area. He disclosed that on 24 February, he closed his shop after news of riots in the evening. The next day, an unknown crowd came and started pelting stones, aiming for his shop. When he heard the sound, he immediately contacted BJP councillor Pramod Gupta and other neighbours, who came forward to help and protect

Mohammad Istar, owner of a unisex salon.

his shop. These goons targeted each and every shop that they came across. In his meeting with us, he has appealed to the people to stay united and maintain peace.

We also met a few people who have played a very important role in extending a helping hand and set an example in the society. Janab Abdul Rashid, aka Haji Babu, vice president of the Residents' Welfare Association (RWA) and president of the Minara Masjid, came forward and extended help to save

Pramod Gupta, councillor, Ghonda, and Abdul Rashid.

people and their property from the violence. He also told us that rioters came from outside, i.e., Chand Bagh and began the destruction.

We met many representatives and members of the Muslim community. We sensed a palpable regret and fear over the incidents that have happened recently in North East Delhi. There is a sense of fear, which is reflected in their refusal to come on camera. Many of them expressed helplessness at how 'outside forces' have exploited their community, resulting in large-scale fatalities and lifelong trauma. Some of the Muslims we met told us how they received messages from the Bhim Army to congregate at Jaffrabad and Bhajanpura to block roads. Messages like these were circulated in Mustafabad and Jaffrabad as well. Many said that tensions in the area intensified after anti-CAA protestors blocked three arterial roads at GT Karnal Road on the Jaffrabad and Chand Bagh side. Muslim residents of the area told us that Kapil Mishra came in after these three roads were blocked.

The Sight of a Riot

We saw evidence of a slew of homemade bombs and launchers, such as huge catapults capable of launching full bricks to distances of up to 300 metres. Can it be pure coincidence that these designs and combat principles used in high-conflict civil war situations like Syria have found their way to localities in the national capital? All these were designed, engineered and manufactured over a long period of time. Nor have they been done without planning, strategy and training.

We saw evidence of pyro-bombardment at all the sites we visited. Such coordinated preparation indicates a very deep and insidious preparation. It hints to the possibility of turning into a national emergency—today or tomorrow. Wilfully choosing to ignore accumulated evidence will only help bring about another exigency.

Catapults used during the riots.

The level and degree to which civil society has been weaponised is a matter of concern. It needs urgent attention to avoid further conflagration.

About the Fact-Finding Team[1]

This fact-finding mission was undertaken by the Group of Intellectuals and Academicians (GIA). Founded in 2015, GIA is a group of professional women and entrepreneurs, media persons and academicians committed to social justice and nation-building.

Members

1. Advocate Monika Arora (Supreme Court of India)
2. Dr Prerna Malhotra, Assistant Professor, Department of English, Ram Lal Anand College (Delhi University)
3. Ms Sonali Chitalkar, Assistant Professor, Department of Political Science, Miranda House (Delhi University)
4. Dr Shruti Mishra, Assistant Professor, Pannalal Girdharlal Dayanand Anglo-Vedic (P.G.D.A.V. [evening]) College (Delhi University)
5. Ms Divyansha Sharma, Assistant Professor, Institute of Home Economics (Delhi University)

---

[1] All photos used throughout the book have been taken by the GIA team.

ANNEXURES

Annexure I: Medical Report – Amit Sharma

MAX HEALTHCARE

Patient Name: Sharma Amit	Location: MAX SUPER SPECIALITY HOSPITAL - PATPARGANJ
Age/Sex: 35/M	IP No.:
Max ID: EHPG 0842971	Admission Type: InPatient
Ref. Doctor: SELF	Order Date: 01-MAR-2020
	Report Date: 02-MAR-2020 10:50 AM

Investigation : NCCT Head

Results : *Contiguous axial sections were taken through the brain without the administration of intravenous contrast.*

Clinical profile: Patient is a post operative case of craniotomy.

Post operative craniectomy changes are seen in the left temporoparietal bone with thickening of overlying scalp.

_____ the underlying brain parenchyma through the craniectomy defect is seen.
Minimal residual extra axial hemorrhage noted in left temporo-parietal region. Few small hemorrhagic contusions are seen in left temporal region and right frontal region.
Few small contusions are also seen in the right temporal region anteriorly.
Rest of the brain parenchyma appears normal.
The cerebellum and IVth ventricle are normal.
Both lateral ventricles and the IIIrd ventricle are normal.
No shift of midline structures is seen.
The basal cisterns, sulci and fissures are normal.

As compared with previous CT scan dated 28th Feb 2020; there is slight decrease in soft tissue swelling overlying left frontotemporoparietal region. no other significant change seen.

Advise : Clinical correlation.

Dr.Vineet Marwaha
'Sr. Consultant

Report Approved / Verified Date & Time:02-MAR-2020 10:50 AM

(For Interpretation by a Registered Medical Practitioner only)

DISCHARGE SUMMARY

PATIENT NAME	: AMIT , SHARMA	AGE/SEX	: 35 Yrs/M
LOCATION NAME	: FPG-IPD NS 7TH FLOOR	SSN NO.	: 080-84-2971
CONSULTANT	: DUA, SANJEEV	DATE OF ADMISSION: Feb 24,2020815:15
ATTEN. PHYSICIAN: DUA, SANJEEV			

Date and Time of Discharge

Mar 4,2020816:00

Diagnosis:

HEAD INJURY WITH LEFT TEMPORO-PARIETAL EDE AND SDH WITH LEFT TEMPORAL CONTUSION

Presenting Complaints:

Patient presented with alleged history of assault by mob at around 1:20 PM on 24/02/2020 and sustained injury to head.
Patient developed swelling in occiptal region, pain in left wrist.
No history of LOC, vomiting, ENT bleed, involuntary movements.

Significant findings during physical examination

CNS: Conscious
GCS: E4 V5 M6
Pupils: Bilateral NSNR
Moving all four limbs

General examination:
BP - 130/80 mmHg
P/R - 96/min
RR- 26/min
Temp- 98.6° F
SPO2- 97% on room air
CVS - S1S2 Normal
RS: B/L, AE Clear
P/A: Soft, BS +

Page 1

For post-hospital care at home, call Max@Home at 8744 888 888 (24x7 helpline).
Services include Critical Care@home, Nursing Care, Healthcare Attendant, Physio-
therapy, X-Ray, Sample Collection, Medicine Delivery, Medical Equipment and more.

IN CASE OF ANY EMERGENCY PLEASE CONTACT 011-40554055

This is a computer generated document and does not require any a signature

Max Super Speciality Hospital, Patparganj - A Unit of Balaji Medical and Diagnostic Research Centre
(Balaji Medical and Diagnostic Research Centre Registered under the Societies Registration Act XXI of 1860)
Regd. Office: 108 A, Indraprastha Extension, Patparganj, New Delhi - 110 092
Phone: +91-11-4303 3333, Fax: +91-11-2223 5563
...maxhealthcare.in

MAX HEALTHCARE

Local Examination:

Big bony swelling in left parito region
Bilateral knee small abrasions
Left wrist tenderness present
Peripheral pulses present

Procedure Performed:

LEFT FTP DECOMPRESSIVE CRANIECTOMY WITH SUCTION AND EVACUATION OF HEMATOMA WITH LEFT ANTERIOR TEMPORAL CONTUSECTOMY DONE ON 25/2/2020

Incision : LEFT FTP QUESTION MARK INCISION MADE

Findings : LEFT TEMPORO-PARIETAL EDH AND SDH WAS PRESENT. BRAIN BULGING PRESENT, BRAIN WAS PULSATION PRESENT. LEFT TEMPORAL CONTUSION WAS PRESENT.

Procedure : AFTER WRITTEN INFORMED CONSENT, PATIENT TAKEN INTO NSOT, PATIENT LAID IN SUPINE POSITION.PATIENT IDENTITY, DIAGNOSIS, SITE AND SIDE CONFIRMED.HEAD TITED TOWARDS RIGHT SIDE. GA ADMINISTERED.QUESTION MARK INCISION WAS MARKED.PAINTING AND DRAPPING DONE. LA INFILTERATED ALONG INCISION LINE.SKIN INCISION MADE AND DEEPENED UPTO BONE. SKIN FLAP RAISED. BURR HOLE MADE. THROUGH BURR HOLE CRANIOTOME WAS USED AND BONE FLAP RAISED. ABOVE MENTIONED FINDINGS WERE PRESENT. SUCTION AND EVACUATION OF HEMATOMA WAS DONE.HITCH SUTURE WAS TAKEN. DURA OPENED, AND THE BRAIN WAS BULGING AND SDH WAS PRESENT. SUCTION AND EVACUATION OF HEMATOMA WAS DONE AND ANTERIOR TEMPORAL CONTUSECTOMY WAS DONE. MEDIAL TEMPORAL LOBE WAS GENTLY LIFTED TO EXPOSE THE TENTORIAL EDGE AND PART OF MEDIAL TEMPORAL LOBE PULLED AWAY FROM TENTORIAL HIATUS TO RELEASE THE Csf. POSTERIOR TEMPORAL CONTUSION LEFT UNTOUCHED AS VEIN OF LABBE'WAS VERY CLOSE AND THE LOBE UNDERLYING IT VERY FRAGILE.BONE KEPT IN BONE BANK.HEMOSTASIS ACHIEVED.BRAIN COVERED WITH G-PATCH. DRAIN PLACED.SKIN AND SUBCUTANEOUS TISSUE CLOSED IN LAYERS. DRESSING DONE ASEPTICALLY.

Course of Hospital:

Patient presented with above mentioned complaints. NCCT Head done showed few small hemorrhagic contusions are seen in left temporal region, extra-axial hematoma seen overlying the cerebral convexity in left temporal region with maximum thickness of approximately 11 mm, there is displacement of underlying rain parenchyma suggesting mass effect, minimal focal extra-axial hemorrhage seen in the right basifrontal region and focal subarachnoid hemorrhage seen along few cerebral sulci in right frontal region, no shift of midline structures is seen, thickening of scalp seen in right parieto-occipital region, fracture of left temporal bone is seen, fracture of the greater wing of sphenoid and adjoining temporal bone seen on right side, non displaced fracture of the right

Page 2

For post-hospital care at home, call Max@Home at 8744 888 888 (24x7 helpline). Services include Critical Care@home, Nursing Care, Healthcare Attendant, Physio-therapy, X-Ray, Sample Collection, Medicine Delivery, Medical Equipment and more.

IN CASE OF ANY EMERGENCY PLEASE CONTACT 011-40554055

"This is a computer generated document and does not require any a signature"

x Super Speciality Hospital, Patparganj - A Unit of Balaji Medical and Diagnostic Research Centre
ψ Medical and Diagnostic Research Centre Registered under the Societies Registration Act XXI of 1860)
Office 108 A, Indraprastha Extension, Patparganj, New Delhi - 110 092
↑ +91-11-4303 3333, Fax: +91-11-2223 5563

Annexure II: Post-mortem Report – Ankit Sharma

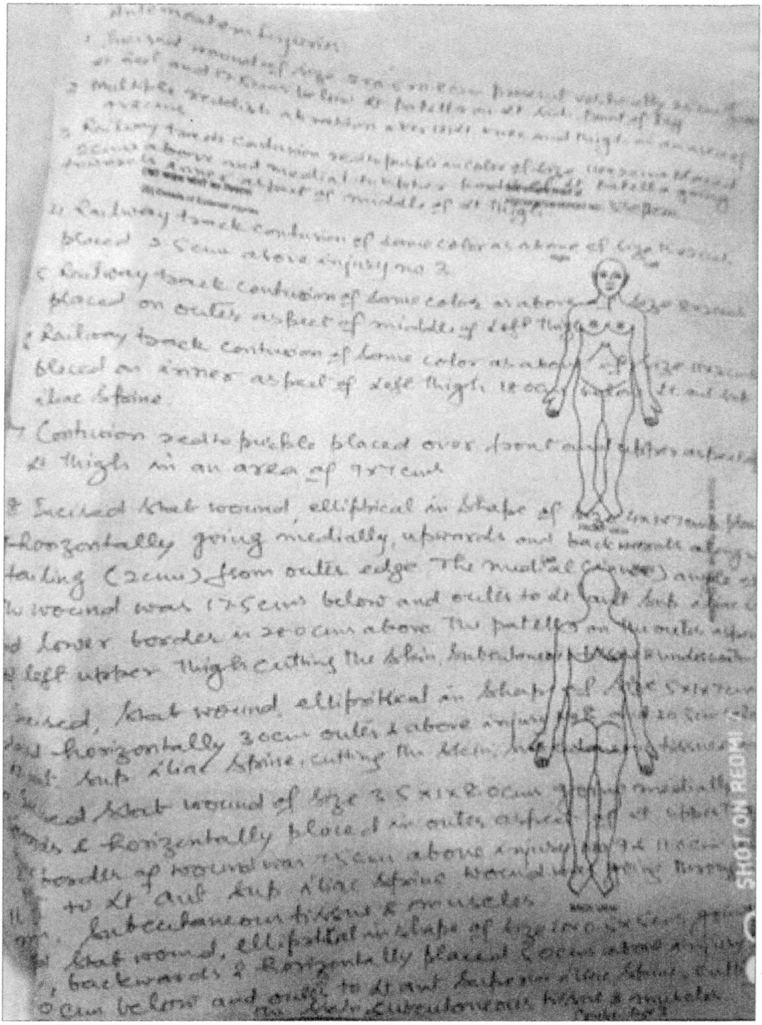

[Handwritten forensic post-mortem injury notes — largely illegible]

Ante-mortem Injuries

1. Incised wound of size ... on ... lower of patella on Lt limb, front of thigh
2. Multiple reddish abrasion over chest, knee and thigh in an area of ...
3. Railway track contusion reddish purple in color of size ... seen above and medial to ... above ... front of middle of Lt thigh
4. Railway track contusion of same color as above of size ... placed 3.5cm above injury no. 2
5. Railway track contusion of same color as above of size ... placed on outer aspect of middle of Left thigh
6. Railway track contusion of same color as above of size ... placed on inner aspect of left thigh it ... iliac bone
7. Contusion red to purple placed over front and ... aspect Lt thigh in an area of 9×7cm
8. Incised stab wound, elliptical in shape of ... horizontally going medially, upwards and backwards ... tailing (2cm) from outer edge. The medial ... angle ... the wound was 17.5cm below and outer to de ... but a ... lower border is 20.0cm above the patella on the outer aspect left upper thigh cutting the skin, subcutaneous ... and underneath
9. Incised, stab wound, elliptical in shape of ... horizontally 30cm outer & above injury ... but iliac spine, cutting the skin ...
10. Incised stab wound of size 3.5×1×2.0cm ... medially and horizontally placed in outer aspect of upper ... border of wound was 7.5cm above injury ... to Lt ant but iliac spine wound ... subcutaneous tissue & muscles
11. ... stab wound, elliptical in shape of size ... backwards & horizontally placed 6 cm above injury ... cm below and outer to Lt ant superior iliac spine, cut ... subcutaneous tissue & muscles

..., area wound, elliptical shaped of size 124.
4.5 x 1 cms x cavity deep, vertically placed 5 cms
outer to midline on Lt side back and 12 cms
below and medial to inf. angle of Lt scapula. 5
The wound 7m going through The skin, 7Th intercostal space & lower lobe of Lt lung (collapsed)
The track was forwards, medially and upward 6

9. Incised, stab wound, elliptical in shape, placed
vertically of size 4x0.8 cm x cavity deep going
forwards, downwards and out wards into The Lt side 7
chest through 7Th Intercostal space placed 1.5cms
above and medial to injury no 18 and 12.5cms
medial & below inferior angle of Lt scapula cutting
w skin, intercostal space with adjacent ribs and
lower lobe of Lt lung (Collapsed)

Red to purple colored contusion all over The outer 9
spect of Lt fore arm of size 18x7 cms.

Red to purple colored contusion present on
outer aspect of Left upper arm & shoulder
of size 36.0 x 10.2 cms, along with reddish abrasions
of size 3 x0.4cm & 3.5 x 0.4cm placed 5 cm below
Lt shoulder tip.

Lacerated wound of size 1x0.2x0.2 cm placed
3.5cms above right medial malleolus on inner aspect
Rt leg.

Red to purple contusion of size 8 x x cm placed in front
Rt leg 5.0 cms, outer & above the medial malleolus
Contd. 5

P.M 230/2020

12. Incised, stab wound, elliptical shaped of size 5x0.5x8cms placed on whatever outer aspect of lt hip 21cm from midline and 60cms post from lt other iliac spine, cutting the skin, subcutaneous tissue & muscle.

13. Incised stab wound, elliptical shaped of size 5x2.5x11.0cms placed obliquely below the lt castal margin onback 8.0cms below the Castal margin and 27.0cms from midline cutting the skin, subcutaneous tissue & muscle going inwards, downwards and horizontally

14. Incised stab wound, elliptical in shape placed vertically of size 3x0.7x5cms going backwards upwards & medially on lt side (backle placed) 5.0cm above injury no 13 cutting the skin subcutaneous tissue & muscles

15. Incised stab wound of size 2.8x0.5x5cms, elliptical in shape placed vertically on lt side back going medially, forwards & horizontally 9.8cms outer to midline and 17.0cms below inferior angle of lt scapula. Wound was involving skin subcutaneous tissue muscle

16. Incised stab wound of size 5x0.8x13.0cms going forwards, medially & downwards, elliptical midshaft Inner angle in 1.0cm from midline and outer placed 6cms below injury no 15. Wound was involving skin, subcutaneous tissue & muscles.

17. Incised wound of size 1x0.2x0.2cm placed on dorsum (back) of lt hand, vertically 3.5cm below the wrist joint and 7.0cm above middle knuckle of ....

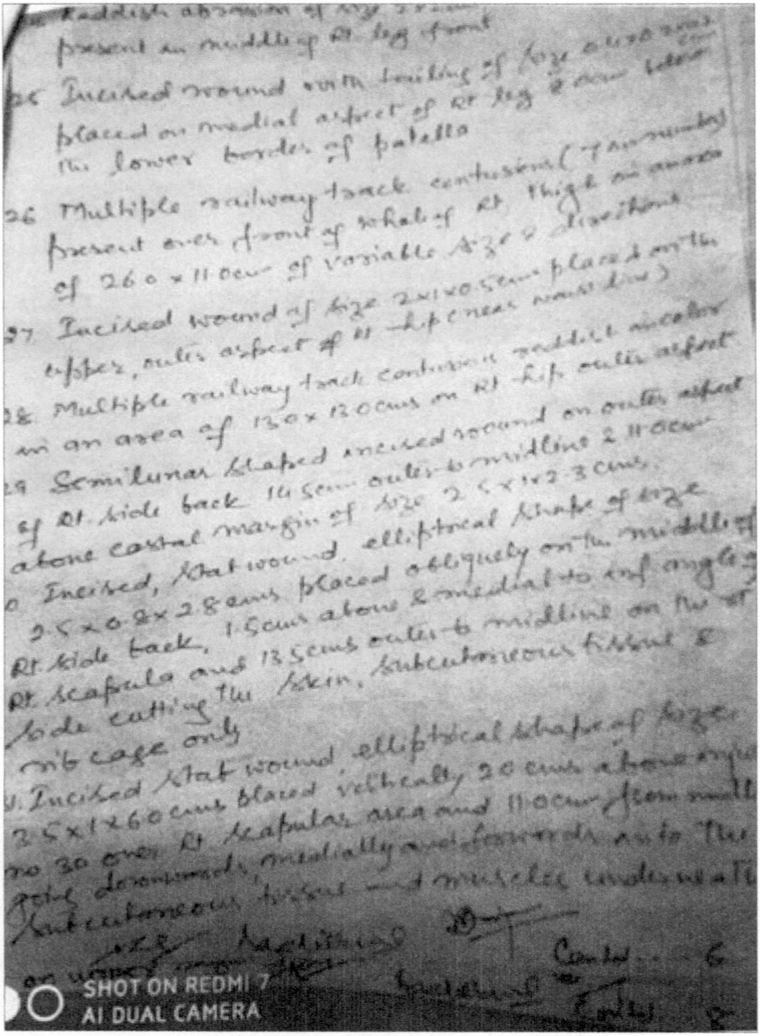

32. 'L' shaped contused lacerated wound with vertical limb 6x0.6x0.5cm and horizontal limb of size 5.5x0.6x0 scms placed on Rt. side occipital area (back of head).

33. Another 'L' shaped contused lacerated wound with vertical limb 10.5x0.5cm x scalp deep and horizontal limb of size 3.5x0.5cm scalp deep placed 1cm above of injury no 32.

34. 'L' shaped contused lacerated wound with vertical limb of size 1x0.5cm scalp deep and horizontal limb of size 1.5x0.5cm x scalp deep placed 6cm away from midline and 4.5cm above Rt ear (pinna)

35. 'V' shaped contused lacerated wound with one limb 2.6 cm and another 2.2 with thickness scalp deep and with 0.5cm placed 8cm from midline and 10cm above & lateral to Rt eye brow on Rt. side head.

36. Linear contused lacerated wound of size 3.8x0.5cm x scalp deep placed on Rt. side head 6cm away from outer angle of Rt eye and 6cm above Rt ear (pinna).

37. Lacerated wound of size 5.8x0.5cm scalp deep vertically placed on Rt. side head 4.5cm above the eye brow and 3.5cm from midline

38. Lacerated wound of size 2.5x0.4cm x scalp deep on Rt. side back of head vertically placed 2 cm on occipital protuberance and 5.5cm above nape of ...

39. Lacerated wound of size 1.2x0.5x1.2cm above occipital protuberance on Rt. side head ...

40. Lacerated ... placed ... wound 8.0cm above ...

Page 7   PM 320/20

• Lacerated wound of size 2.5×0.5cm × scalp deep placed vertically on Lt. side back of head 5.5cm away from midline and 6.0cm above the occiput

11. Lacerated wound of size 4×0.5cm × scalp deep placed obliquely 4.0cm from midline and 2.5cm above occiput on Lt side back of head

12 Incised wound (chop) wound horizontally on Rt. side forehead of size 3.0×1.0×cavity deep (cms) placed 2.0cm to the Rt of midline (inner angle) and 7.8cm medial to Rt ear (outer angle), having cut fracture of the underline bone with vault 7.5cm in length and diameter also showing torn/cut

13 Lacerated wound of size 1.8×0.5cm×scalp deep present just above outer angle of Rt upper eye lid.

14. Lacerated wound of size 2.5×0.5cm × muscle deep placed just below the medial end of Rt eye brow.

15 'L' shaped lacerated wound of size 3 (V)×3× bone deep (cms) placed obliquely over Rt side of nose

16 Lacerated wound of size 7×3.5cm × scalp deep placed obliquely starting just above Lt eye brow going upto temporal region.

17 Reddish abrasion of size 2×1cm placed on outer as of Rt upper eye lid.

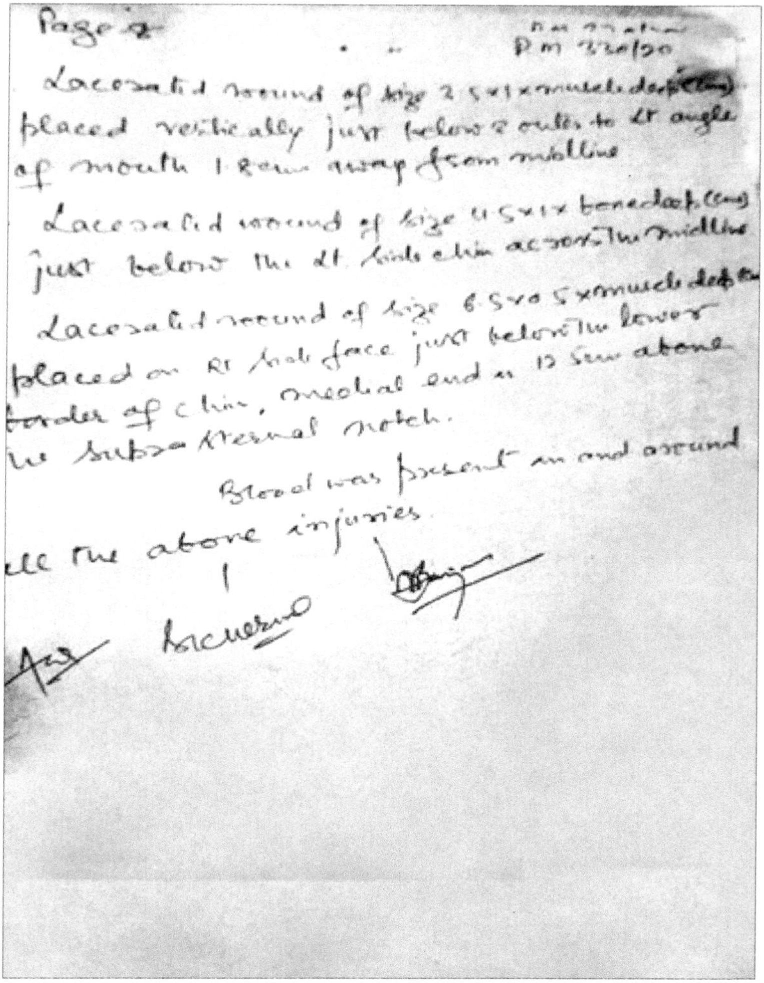

Page 2

P.m. 330/20

Lacerated wound of size 2.5×1×muscle deep (cm) placed vertically just below & outer to Lt angle of mouth 1.8cm away from midline

Lacerated wound of size 4.5×1× bone deep (cm) just below the Lt limb chin across the midline

Lacerated wound of size 6.5×0.5×muscle deep (cm) placed on Rt half face just below the lower border of chin, medial end is 13.5cm above the substernal notch.

Blood was present in and around all the above injuries.

(40)

पोस्टमार्टम रिपोर्ट सं. 330/20

(घ) रासायनिक विश्लेषण के लिए रखे गए सूचियन नमूने (यदि लागू हो) — —

(ड) परिरक्षी प्रयोग में लाया गया — —

(च) कपड़े/अन्य सूचियन रखे गई वस्तुएं (यदि कोई हो)
① Clothes
⑤ Blood or gauge

(छ) विशेषतायें (यदि कोई हो) — vedeography of the case was got done by IO

Time Since Death: About 2 (Two) days

(ज) राय — Cause of death is shock due to haemorrhage due to injury to lung & Brain bearing no 18, 19, 34-37 & 42 All these injuries were sufficient to cause death in ordinary course of nature both independently and collectively. Further injuries no 1, 8-19, 25, 27, 29-3) were produced by sharp edged weapon, while injury no 42 was produced by heavy cutting weapon and rest were by blunt force. All injuries were fresh before death (i.e with in 24 hours).

हस्ताक्षर व पदनाम करने वाले चिकित्सा अधिकारी
Signature & Designation of Medical Officer

(Dr. X K Banerjee)

(Dr. SK Verma)

पुलिस को दी गई वस्तुएं
Item handed over to police

1. जांच पड़ताल में कागजात/inquest/papers Total ② eight sheet only
2. मूल पोस्टमार्टम रिपोर्ट Postmortem report in original

प्राप्तकर्ता पुलिस जांच अधिकारी का नाम
Name of receiving police investigation officer

ASI Rajinder kumar 2034E

1- Dayal Pur Delhi
2/3/2020
P.S 28834105

Police Station
Dayal Por...

DOPGPF—229 GTB/40017—24.09.2017—1 का Pads

Annexure III: Riots in Eastern Range

RIOT from 15.12.19 to 22.02.2020 in Eastern Range

District	Cases registered
Shahdara	01
East	00
North-East	06
Eastern Range	07

North-East Distt:- 06

1. Dayal Pur :-02
2. Seelam Pur:-01
3. Jafrabad :-01
4. Nand Nagri:-01
5. Khajuri Khas:01

Shahdara District :-01

Seema Puri:-01

Shahdara   Rep-01   W/o- 01

FIR No.	Date and U/S	Police Station	Brief Facts	Details of arrested accused person
816	20.12.19 u/s 307/143/147/148/149/186/353 /109 IPC & 3/4 DPDP Act	Seema Puri	Complainant HC Sunil Kumar No. 276//Shd. reported that on 20.12.2019 at 1545 hrs about 1000-1500 persons in the leadership of Haji Tahir Siddiqi gathered at Seema Puri started pelting stone on Police Staff in which some police personnel got injured. (14 persons arrested)	Sadi s/o Lorak r/o C-345, Sohad Nagar Ghaziabd, Rajaulah Khan s/o Shahbuddin r/o B-523, Sohad Nagar Ghaziabd, Mohd. Sonu s/o Bagadat r/o B-13, Kallan Chowk, Sohad Nagar Ghaziabd, Nisar s/o Asab Mohammad r/o E-68, Old Seema Puri, Aziz s/o Sageer r/o B-196, Moti Masjid, Sohad Nagar Ghaziabd, Wajer s/o Nawur Ahmad r/o B-121, Old Seema Puri, Amruddin s/o Salimuddin r/o C-153, Sohad Nagar Ghaziabd, Abdul Kalam s/o Abdul Majid r/o A-316, Old Seema Puri, Amjad Khan s/o Yameen r/o L-9, Gali No. 12, Brahan Puri, Armaad Ahmad s/o Anjar r/o P-18/19, Old Seema Puri, Haji Mehraj s/o Abdul Majeed r/o A-113/114, Old Seema Puri arrested on 21.12.19 and Aslam s/o Mehfooj r/o A-42, Old Seema Puri arrested on 24.12.19 and Shaukat Ali s/o Mohd. Ali r/o A-295, Shahara Nagar, Ghaziabad, U.P. and Nuruddeen s/o Musttaten Ansari r/o A-324, Old Seema Puri arrested on 25.12.19

North-East-734

Sl. No.	FIR No.	Date and U/S	Police Station	Brief Facts	Details of arrested accused person
1	510	16.12.19 u/s 186/353/3 32/147/14 8/149 IPC & 3 DPDP Act	Dayal Pur	Complainant HC Sunil PIS No. 28901272 P.S. Dayal Pur, Delhi reported that on 16.12.19 at 08.15 PM during patrolling on information received that some persons stopped the traffic and opposed the NRC & CAB Bill. SHO & staff reached the spot and found gathering of about 60-70 persons and they were violent and damaged government properties. They also pelted stones due to which some police persons injured in this protest.	Mohd. Arbaz Malik s/o Mohd. Hanif r/o F-7, Gali No. 1, Chand Bagh, Asthag Alam s/o Firoz Alam r/o F-80, Gali No. 3, Chand Bagh and Matin Ansari s/o Bearuddin r/o House of Imran ka Karkhana, Gali No. 1, A-Block, Chand Bath Dayal Pur arrested on 17.12.19
2	535	17.12.19 u/s 147/148/1 49/186/35 3/332/30 7/435 IPC & 3/4 PDPP Act	Seelam Pur	Complainant Inspr. Manoj Kumar, SHO/Seelam Pur reported that on 17.12.19 some persons were on protest against NRC & CAB. Due to the possibility of protest march the staff was deployed near T-Point, 66 Ft. Road, where a huge number of persons had gathered. They were warned that the obstacles caused to traffic is unlawful but all in vain. During the dispersal the crowd indulged in stone pelting. They damaged a police booth at Road No. 66 and set ablaze to private vehicles. They raised anti police slogans. To control the mob, some bullets were fired in air and tear gas also used. (12 persons arrested)	*(illegible list of 12 arrested persons)*
3	699	17.12.19 u/s 147/148/1 49/186/35 3/332/30 7/427/43 5/120-B IPC & 3/4 PDPP Act	Jafrabad	Complainant Inspr. Lekh Raj Singh, SHO Jafrabad reported that on 17.12.19 40-50 persons organized a bike rally led by Sh. Matin Ahmed, Ex. MLA, Seelam Pur against NRC & CAB without permission. They raised anti CAB & NRC slogans. Huge public gathered near T-Point, Seelam Pur, Road No. 66, and started pelting stones, bricks and patrol bombs upon police personals. Resulting some police personals sustained injuries. They damaged some vehicles and set ablaze a public portable toilet and broke the glass of a car.	*(illegible list of arrested persons)*

4	512	18.12.19 u/s 147/148/14 9/186/353/ 332/427/4 32/34 IPC & 3/4 PDPP Act	Dayal Pur	Inspector Tarkeshwar, SHO/Dayalpur stated that he along with other police personnel were present tat Brijpuri T- Point, some persons of the locality started rally w/o permission against the implementation of CAA 2019. They gathered at Brij Puri T-point and started pelting stones on police personnel.	Mohd. Nazim s/o Mohd. Islamuddin r/o 6-208, Gali No. 13/7, Prem Dr. Wali Gali Bhagirathi Vihar arrested on 18.12.19
5	760	20.12.19 u/s 186/353/3 32/147/14 8/149/188 IPC	Nand Nagri	Ct. Ramesh No. 1107/NE stated that on 20.12.19 he was deployed on arrangement duty in Sunder Nagri area with other staff. Section 144 Cr.P.C. was imposed there but some people started stone plating on us. For stop them we took primary steps and tear gas in this conflict SHO/Harsh Vihar and other police staff sustained injury.	Imran s/o Anser r/o Khasno Colony Gali No. 3, Ghaziabad, Aspel s/o Shubhan Khan r/o Khasno Colony GLF Ghaziabad, Babli s/o Monjid r/o E-43, New Seema Puri, Farhan s/o Anser r/o Khasno Colony, Gali No. 3, Ghaziabade, Rafi s/o Nasar r/o Khasno Colony, Gali No. 3, Ghaziabad, and Mehtab s/o munafin r/o Khasno Colony Gali No. 3 Ghaziabad, UP arrested on 20.12.19 and Nadeem s/o Isafiquddin r/o 1-354, Sunder Nagri, Wasseem s/o Mohd. Dilyesh r/o H-571, Sunder Nagri, Asif s/o Abid r/o O-116, Sudner Nagri, Mandeli, Adil s/o Abid r/o C-124, Gali No. 7, Rajeev Nagar, Gulgar s/o Asgar Ali r/o F-II/354, Sunder Nagar and Shahrukh s/o Shamsuddin r/o E-117/74, Sunder Nagri arrested on 21.12.19 and Shaikh s/o Taj Ahmed r/o Flat No. 1569, Tulsi Niketan Ghaziabad arrected on 22.12.19
6	83	11.2.2020 u/s 186/353/3 32/109/34 1/283/427 /341/147/ 148/149 IPC & 3 DPDP Act	Khajuri Khas	Complainant SI Arun Kumar reported that during patrolling when he reached at F-Block, there he noticed some gathering and found that one dead body of boy was lying side of drain (nala) The child was missing from some day before and a FIR 80/2020 was registered u/s 363 IPC in Ps Khajur Khas and his parents demanded that they remove it only when media and politicians visit there. He exhorted them a lot but they did not agree and due to this the way was blocked completely and he did video-grapy of this incident. After senior officer reached there they agreed to took that child dead body to Hospital for postmortem and after postmortem when he was returning in his vehicle then he left behind the ambulance due to traffic. When he reached there he found that the parents of child made unlawful assembly and blocked the traffic, injured the public and police by pelting bricks and stone on them and sabotaged and damaged the private and Govt. vehicles.	Amit s/o Ram Avtar r/o K-181/2, Sadat Pur Extn. arrested on 9.3.2020

Annexure IV: Post-mortem Report – Ratan Lal

DEPARTMENT OF FORENSIC MEDICINE,
UCMS & GURU TEG BAHADUR HOSPITAL, DELHI -110095
POSTMORTEM No. 114 /2020

Date and Time of receiving dead body for Post mortem — 25/02/2020 at 11:00AM
Date and Time of starting Autopsy — 25/02/2020 at 11:10AM
Date and Time of concluding Autopsy — 25/02/2020 at 12:35PM

Body brought and identified by:
Name of Investigating Officer ASI Hira Lal, PS - Dayal Pur, Delhi
Body Also identified by:
1) Manoj S/O Brij Mohan R/O Vill. & P.O. Thawali, Dist. Sikar, Rajasthan (Brother)
2) Bhanwar Lal S/O Late Sh. Hardat R/O 038/3 Padam Nagar, Sarai Rohila, Delhi (Cousin Brother)

Name of Deceased   Ratan Lal S/O Brij Mohan R/O 1E 17 A Block, Gali No-8, Burari,
Delhi Age: 43yrs   Sex: Male

Brief History of the case (as per inquest papers): It was alleged that he was assaulted by mob when he was on duty on 24/02/2020. He was brought to GTB Hospital where he was declared dead vide MLC no BD5537/02/2020 on 24/02/2020 at 2:12PM

Length 171 St. ms   **Weight:** Machine not in function.

General Observations:
    Dead body of an adult male with good body built, wrapped in a white plastic sheet. He was wearing Khakhi color Shirt which having Delhi Police emblem (Red and Blue color) and two chevrons over both sleeves. Khakhi color pant (Delhi police Uniform), Navy blue color thermal (upper and lower), sleeveless banyan, nikker type underwear (Dixy Scott printed on it), white handkerchief and pair of navy blue color woollen gloves. Dry blood stains were present at places over uniform, over scalp hairs, face and hands. A circular hole was present over left sleeve of shirt and inner, which was encircled. Clothes were removed, preserved and sealed. Eyes and mouth were partially open. Post mortem staining was present over the back except pressure area and fixed. Rigor mortis was present all over the limbs. Blue ink stain was present over thumbs of both hands. Injection prick mark was present over left cubital fossa. Body was sent for X-Ray examination at 11.44AM and came back at 12.10PM. X-Ray plate showed a metallic object over right arm. X-Ray plates were initialled and returned to Radiology department.

Details of External Examination:
1. Oval shape firearm entry wound of size 1.2cm X 1cm placed lateral aspect of left upper arm, 6cm away from tip of left shoulder and 12.5cm away and above to left anterior axillary fold and 149cm above left heel. An abrasion collar was present over the antero-lateral margin of the wound. On dissection of the wound, the underlying left humerus bone was fractured. direction of the track was downward, backward and left to right, track entered the left chest cavity after fracturing the 3rd rib at anterior axillary line, passing through and through to the apical lobe of left lung, body of L3 vertebrae and apical lobe of right lung, then exit the right chest cavity after fracturing 4th rib up and then to the posterior muscles of right arm where a copper jacketed bullet of size 1.5cm in length and 0.8cm diameter of base was found. Total length of the track was 48cm. Bullet was removed, preserved and sealed after making an X mark on the base. Both chest cavities were filled with blood and blood clots of about 1 litre.
2. Reddish abrasion of size 0.5cm X0.5cm present over dorsal aspect of left hand, 3.5cm above the knuckle of index finger.
3. Reddish abrasion of size 0.3cm X0.3cm present over knuckles of middle and ring fingers of left hand.
4. Reddish abrasion of size 1cm X0.4cm present over dorsal aspect of ring finger of right hand.

DEPARTMENT OF FORENSIC MEDICINE,
UCMS & GURU TEG BAHADUR HOSPITAL, DELHI -110095

POSTMORTEM No. 314 /2020

5. Reddish abrasion of size 0.5cm X 0.5cm present over dorsal aspect of middle finger of right hand.

6. Lacerated wound of size 1cm X0.1cm X muscles deep present over medial phalanx of middle finger of right hand.

7. Reddish abrasion of size 1.5cm X 1cm present over left upper eyelid with underlying bruise of size 1cm X 2cm.

8. Reddish abrasion of size 2cm X 1cm obliquely placed, present over left side of head, 5.5cm away from midline and 3.5cm above left eyebrow.

9. Reddish abrasion of size 2.5cm X 0.4cm, horizontally placed, present over left side of forehead, 5cm away from midline and 5.5cm above lateral margin of left eyebrow.

10. Reddish bruise of size 4cm X 3cm present over the middle of forehead placed across the midline.

11. Reddish abrasion of size 0.5cm X 0.3cm present over antihelix of left ear.

12. Reddish abrasion with reddish bruise of size 3.5cm X 0.5cm, horizontally placed, present over left ear, below left ear lobe.

13. Lacerated wound of size 2.5cm X0.5cm X bone deep present over right occipito-parieto-temporal area, 10cm above to the tip of right mastoid and 9.5cm right from midline.

14. Lacerated wound of size 1.2cm X0.5cm X bone deep present over right head, 1cm above and behind to the injury no 13.

15. Lacerated wound of size 5cm X 1cm X bone deep, horizontally placed, present over the left parietal area, medial end was not on midline and lateral end was 16cm above to the tip of left mastoid.

16. Lacerated wound of size 2.5cm X0.5cm X bone deep, horizontally placed, present over occipital protuberance.

17. Reddish abrasion of size 2cm X 0.6cm present over patella of left knee.

18. Reddish abrasion of size 2.5cm X2cm present over the anterior aspect of right leg,10cm below the right patella.

19. Reddish abrasion of size 1.2cm X0.5cm present over the anterior aspect of right leg, 22cm below the right patella.

20. Reddish tram track bruise of size 6cm X2.5cm with intervening normal skin of size1cm, obliquely placed over the posterior aspect of right leg, 9cm below right knee joint.

21. Reddish abrasion of size 0.5cm X 0.5cm present over right popliteal fossa.

Details of Internal Examination:

Head and Neck
Scalp: Extravasation of blood was present over both parietal, temporal and right frontal area.
Skull: NAD
Brain: Edema, oedematous and diffuse sub arachnoid haemorrhage was present more on left cerebrum and cerebellum.

Neck and Vertebrae: NAD

Chest (Thorax)
Rib Cage: as mentioned above
Lungs: Right 260gms, left 220gms. Injury as mentioned above.
Heart: Weighs 240gms. All coronaries were patent.

Abdomen and Others
Stomach: Contains 50 ml of brownish color fluid. Walls: NAD.
Intestine: NAD Walls: NAD
Spleen: weighs 80gms, pale
Liver: Weighs 1130gms, pale
Kidney: Right 110gms, left 85gms pale
Urinary bladder: Empty Wall- NAD

DEPARTMENT OF FORENSIC MEDICINE,
UCMS & GURU TEG BAHADUR HOSPITAL, DELHI -110095
POSTMORTEM No. 314 /2020

Articles preserved:
1. Clothes as mentioned above
2. Blood on gauze piece
3. Bullet recovered from the body

All above articles were sealed with the seal "AK" and handed over to IO.

OPINION

Time since death is about one day.
Cause of death-Haemorrhagic shock as result of ante mortem injury to lungs produced by projectile of rifled firearm. All injuries were ante mortem in nature. Injury No 1 was produced by projectile of firearm. Injury no 2 to 21 were produced by blunt force impact object. Injuries no 1, 10, 13, 14, 15 and 16 were sufficient to cause death in ordinary course of nature independently and collectively.

Dr. Arvind Kumar 2/2/20
Assistant Professor
Department of Forensic Medicine

Items handed over to police:

1. Inquest papers total 8 (Eight)
2. Post-mortem report in original

Name of receiving police constable officer Insp Tavipeshwor singh No - D-J/472

Police station

16 10 012 G.

Signature: Singh 7/3/20.

(3/3)

Annexure V: FIRs

FIRST INFORMATION REPORT
(Under Section 154 Cr.P.C.)

(धारा 154 दंड प्रक्रिया संहिता के तहत)

1. District (जिला): CENTRAL   P.S (थाना): DARYA GANJ   Year (वर्ष): 2019   FIR No.(प्रा.सू.रि.सं.): 003/36   Date : 21/12/2019

2. Act(s)(अधिनियम):   Section(s)(धाराएं):
   - IPC 1860   147/148/149/436/427/323/180/353/333/1208/34
   - PREVENTION OF DAMAGE TO PUBLIC   3/4
     PROPERTY ACT 1984

3. Occurrence of Offence (अपराध की घटना):
   (a) Day(दिन):   FRIDAY   Date From(दिनांक से): 20/12/2019   Date To(दिनांक तक):   20/12/2019
       Time Period (समय अवधि):   Time From (समय से):   18:00 hrs   Time To (समय तक):   18:00 hrs
   (b) Information received at P.S.(थाना जहां सूचना प्राप्त हुई):   Date(दिनांक): 21/12/2019   Time (समय): 01:11 hrs
   (c) General Diary Reference (दैनंदिनी संदर्भ):   Entry No.(प्रविष्टि सं.): 004A   Time (समय): 01:11 hrs

4. Type of Information (सूचना का प्रकार):   Written

5. Place of Occurrence (घटनास्थान):
   (a) Direction and Distance from P.S (थाना से दूरी और दिशा): SOUTH-WEST , 0.1 Km(s)   Beat No(बीट सं.) : 09
   (b) Address(पता): ,IN FRONT OF DCP OFFICE & PS DARYA GANJ N S MARG DARYA GANJ DELHI
   (c) In case, Outside the limit of the Police Station (यदि थाना सीमा के बाहर है):
       Name of P.S(थाना का नाम):   District(जिला):

6. Complainant / Informant (शिकायतकर्ता/सूचनाकर्ता):
   (a) Name(नाम): RAKESH KUMAR SHARMA
   (b) Date/Year of Birth (जन्म तिथि /वर्ष): 17/10/1968   Nationality (राष्ट्रीयता):   INDIA
   (c) Passport No.(पासपोर्ट सं.):   Date of Issue (जारी करने की तिथि):   Place of Issue (जारी करने का स्थान):
   (d) Occupation (व्यवसाय):
   (e) Address(पता):   A-3, TYPE-III, NEW POLICE COLONY, MODEL TOWN, NORTH WEST DELHI, 110009,
       INDIA, 8750870421, SHO.DARYAGANJ@DELHIPOLICE.GOV.IN

7. Details of Known/Suspect/Unknown accused with full particulars(attach separate sheet if necessary)(ज्ञात/संदिग्ध /अज्ञात अभियुक्त का
   का पूरे विवरण सहित वर्णन):

8. Reason for delay in reporting by the complainant/informant (शिकायतकर्ता / सूचनाकर्ता द्वारा रिपोर्ट देरी से दर्ज करने के कारण).
   NO DELAY

9. Particulars of the properties stolen/involved (attach separate sheet if necessary):

   Sl.No. (क्र.सं.) Property Type(Description)   Est. Value(Rs.)(मूल्य (रु में))
      1   AUTOMOBILES AND OTHERS(CAR NO DL 5CQ 9038)

District : CENTRAL   P.S. GARYA GANJ   Year: R/9   F.IR No: 0250   Date : 21/12/19

10.Total value of property stolen (चोरी हुई सम्पति का कुल मूल्य):

11.Inquest Report / U.D. Case No., if any (मृत्यु समीक्षा रिपोर्ट / यू.डी.प्रकरण न., यदि कोई हो):

12.F.I.R. Contents (attach separate sheet, if required)(प्रथम सूचना रिपोर्ट तथ्य):

Statement of INSP. Rakesh Kumar Sharma D- I/541 SHO/Darya ganj Delhi. Age 51 years बयान किया कि मै थाना दरियागंज मे बतौर INSP./SHO कार्यरत हूँ जो दिनाक 19/12/19 को Mr. Chander Shakher @ Ravan , भीम आर्मी के मुख्य नेता के द्वारा Citizenship Amendment Act तथा National Register of Citizens के recent Amendment के विरोध मे Walled city area मे जामा मस्जिद आदरे दिनाक 20/12/19 को जबरदस्ती Protest करने कि धमकी दी थी । जो इस धमकी के मद्देनगर Walled city area और उसके आस पास शान्ति व्यवस्था बनाये रखने के लिये और Law and order को maintain करने के लिये Force को Properly Deploy किया गया था जो मै खुद Staff व अन्य Senior Officers के साथ Law & order maintain करने के लिये N S Marg पर तैनात था । जो दिनाक 20/12/19 को Jama Masjid मे Friday prayer के दौरान Mr. Chander Shakher @ Ravan , भीम आर्मी के मुख्य नेता के द्वारा भड़काउ भाषण दिये गये जिससे कई हजार लोगो कि भीड़ जामा मस्जिद से दिल्ली गेट की तरफ इकठ्ठा होने लगी जिनको Delhi gate पर barricading करके रोकने कि कोशिश कि गई और भीड़ को Loud hailer द्वारा वापस लौट जाने के लिये आगाह किया गया और मस्जिद मे ऐलानिया तौर पर भीड़ को वापस जाने के लिये कहा गया । जो धीरे धीरे लोगो का हुजूम वापस लौटने लगा । जो समय करीब 6 बजे शाम सूचना मिली की North east District Delhi से 4 से 5 हजार लोगो का हुजूम आ रहा है जो देखते ही देखते अचानक दिल्ली गेट के पास DCP Office, Central District व थाना Darya ganj के बाहर अचानक 8 से 10 हजार लोगो कि भीड़ इकठ्ठा हो गई । जो इस भीड़ मे मौजूद सभी लोग Citizen ship Amendment Act तथा National Register of Citizens के recent Amendment के विरोध मे केन्द्र सरकार के खिलाफ नारे लगा रहे थे तथा जनता के जाने के लिये उग्र हो रहे थे । जिनको Senior Officers के द्वारा शान्ति बनाये रखने तथा Law and order को maintain करने के लिये समझाया गया जो नही माने तथा मस्जिद मे ऐलान कराने के बाद भी भीड़ मौके से नही हट रही थी और उग्र होती जा रही थी तथा नारे लगा रही थी जो अचानक भीड़ ने पुलिस पार्टी पर पथराव करना शुरू कर दिया । जब पुलिस पार्टी के समझाने पर भी भीड़ तितर बितर नही हुई इसलिये उग्र भीड़ पर water canon से पानी कि बौछार की गई लेकिन लोगो की उग्र भीड़ ने सड़क पर खड़ी एक Car No. DL 5CQ 3038 मे आग लगा दी । जो मन INSP. ने इसकी सूचना C-50 Control Room को दी । जब काफी समझाने के बाद भी उग्र भीड़ नही मानी तो मौजूदा पुलिस बल ने Senior Officer के आदेश पर Minimum जायज Force का इस्तेमाल करते हुये लोगो को दिल्ली गेट से खदेड़ना शुरू किया जिसमे कई लोगो को गिरने कि वजह से भी चोटे आई है तथा कई पुलिस कर्मी उग्र भीड़ के पत्थराव से घायल हुये है । जो मुझे भी पेट मे पत्थराव/डण्डा लगने से चोट लगी है जो इस प्रकार जायज Force का इस्तेमाल करते हुये उग्र भीड़ पर काबू पाया गया । यदि पुलिस द्वारा जायज Force ना किया जाता तो उग्र भीड़ इससे भी अधिक जान और माल को नुकसान पहुंचा सकती थी जो पुलिस बल द्वारा मौका से काफी लोगो को Detain किया गया है जिनसे पुछताछ अमल मे लाई जा रही है जो इस प्रकार उग्र भीड़ मे उपस्थित प्रदर्शनकारियो ने बिना Permission इकठ्ठा होकर Common Object के तहत Unlawful assembly बनाकर व Unlawful assembly के Members बने रहकर तैनात पुलिस बल को उनकी Official Duty मे बाधा पहुँचाकर व ईट - पत्थरो से हमला करके Private & Public Property को Damage किया है लिहाजा कानूनी कार्यवाही की जावे जो इस सम्बन्ध मे आप हाजिर LNJP Hospital आये । आपने मेरा Statement record किया है जो मैने पढ़ा सुना ठिक है Sd English (Rakesh Kr. Sharma) SHO/Darya ganj Attested SI Mukesh Tomar PS Darya ganj Delhi Dt 21/12/19 श्रीमान Duty Officer PS Darya ganj Delhi निवेदन इस प्रकार है कि दिनाक 20/12/19 को मै Law & Order duty पर था व Night Emergency Duty 8 PM to 8 AM भी perform कर रहा था । जो मन SI को GD no. 85A मिलने पर मन SI समय CT Baljeet No. 1003/C जाय मौका पहुंची जहाँ पर काफी Injured का Hospital जाना मालूम हुआ व मौका पर FSL व Crime team को सुलाया गया जो LNJP Hospital पँहुचने पर MLC No. 113665033 बनाने Rakesh Kumar Sharma S/O Lt. Sh. S K Sharma PS Darya ganj Age 51 years हासिल की जिस पर Dr. Sir ने A/H/O Hit by wooden slick by protester at around 6.15 PM as told by Patient it self and nature of injury U/O लिखा व काफी अन्य Police Officer का बैरे इलाज होना मालूम हुआ जिनकी Detail collect की जा रही है Insp Rakesh Kumar Sharma का बयान हासिल किया जो हालात से व DD Entry के Content से Offence under U/S 147/148/149/188/353/332/323/427/435/120B/34 IPC & ¼ PDPP Act का होना पाया गया जो मन SI ने एक तहरीर तैयार की जो दर्पेश है । FIR दर्ज करके Number of FIR बताया जाये मन SI जाय मौका का रवाना होता है । date & Time of Occurrence – 20/12/19 at about 6 PM place of occurrence – in front of DCP Office & PS Darya ganj N S Marg Darya ganj Delhi Date & time of producing the Tahrir – 21/12/19 at 1 am Sd English SI

2

| District: CENTRAL | P.S: DARYA GANJ | Year: 2019 | FIR No: 0050 | | Date: 21/12/2019 |

Mukesh Tomar No. D-4850 PS Darya ganj Delhi Dt 21/12/19 पुलिस कार्यवाही अज थाना SI Mukesh Tomar D-4850 ने हाज़िर Duty Officer Room आकर मन ASI/DO को एक हिन्दी तहरीर दरवेश की जो तहरीर की दरपेशगी पर मुक़दमा U/S 147/148/149/436/427/323/186/353/332/120B/34 IPC & ¾ PDPP Act का CCTNS Operator द्वारा Computer में Feed कराया गया व असल तहरीर व FIR Computerized Copy and Certificate U/S 65 Evidence Act. बदस्त CT Baljeet No. 1003/C द्वारा SI Mukesh Tomar D-4850 के पास भिजवाई गई जो मौक़ा पर मशरूफ व तफ़्तीश है। दीगर काग़ज़ात व नक़ूलात बज़रीये हाल अफ़सरान वाला की खिदमत में अरसाल है By/DO

13. Action Taken Since the above information reveals commission of offence(s) u/s as mentioned at item No. 2:
(की गयी कार्यवाही: चूंकि उपरोक्त जानकारी से पता चलता है कि किया गया अपराध मद सं.2.में उल्लेख धारा के तहत है):

(i) Registered the case and took up the investigation: OR (या)
(पंजीकरण दर्ज किया गया और जांच के लिए लिया गया):

(ii) Directed (Name of the I.O.)(जांच अधिकारी का नाम): MUKESH KUMAR Rank (पद):
SI (SUB-INSPECTOR)

No(सं.): 28061422 to take up the investigation (को जांच आगे पास में लेने के लिए निर्देश दिया गया) OR(या)
OR (के कारण इंकार किया या)

(iii) Refused investigation due to(जांच के लिए):

(iv) Transferred to P.S(name)(थाना): District(जिला):
on point of jurisdiction (को क्षेत्राधिकार के कारण हस्तांतरित)

F.I.R read over to the complainant/informant,admitted to be correctly recorded and a copy given to the complainant/informant, free of cost : (शिकायतकर्ता / सूचनाकर्ता को शिकायती पढ़ कर सुनाई गयी, सही दर्ज हुई माना और एक कॉपी निःशुल्क शिकायतकर्ता को दी गयी) :

R.O.A.C.(आर.ओ.ए.सी.):

14. Signature / Thumb Impression
of the Complainant / Informant:
(शिकायतकर्ता / सूचनाकर्ता के हस्ताक्षर / अंगूठे का निशान):

Signature of Officer
Name(नाम): UDAY BIR SINGH
Rank (पद): ASST. SI (ASSISTANT SUB-INSPECTOR)
No.(सं.): 28912096

15. Date and Time of despatch to the court:
(अदालत में देश को भेजने की दिनांक और समय):

FIRST INFORMATION REPORT
(Under Section 154 Cr.P.C.)

(धारा 154 दंड प्रकिया संहिता के तहत)

1. District (जिला):SOUTH　　　P.S.(थाना): SAKET　　　Year(वर्ष): 2020　FIR No(प्र.सू.रि.सं.):0070　　　Date :24/02/2020

2. Act(s)(अधिनियम):
- IPC 1860　　　　　Section(s)(धाराएं):
143/147/148/149/186/353/332/120B/34

3. Occurrence of Offence (अपराध की घटना):
(a) Day(दिन):　SUNDAY　　　Date From(दिनांक से): 23/02/2020　　Date To(दिनांक तक):　23/02/2020
Time Period (समय अवधि):　　Time From (समय से): 19:00 hrs　　Time To (समय तक):　19:00 hrs
(b) Information received at P.S.(थाना जहां सूचना प्राप्त हुई):　Date(दिनांक): 24/02/2020　　　Time (समय): 14:19 hrs
(c) General Diary Reference (रोजनामचा संदर्भ):　　Entry No.(प्रविष्टि सं.): 024A　Date/Time(दिनांक/समय): 24/02/2020 14:19

4. Type of Information (सूचना का प्रकार):　Written

5. Place of Occurrence (घटनास्थल):
(a) Direction and Distance from P.S (थाना से दूरी और दिशा): WEST , 1.0　Km(s)　　　　Beat No(बीट सं.) : 02
(b) Address(पता):　MAIN PRESS ENCLAVE ROAD ,OPPOSITE MAX SMART HOSPITAL　NEAR ,GANDHI PARK HAUZ RANI SAKET,
DELHI
(c) In case, Outside the limit of the Police Station (यदि थाना सीमा के बाहर है):
Name of P.S(थाना का नाम):　　　　　District(जिला):

6. Complainant / Informant (शिकायतकर्ता/सूचनाकर्ता):
(a) Name(नाम): CT BABULAL
(b) Date/Year of Birth (जन्म तिथि /वर्ष):　　　　Nationality (राष्ट्रीयता):　INDIA
(c) Passport No.(पासपोर्ट सं.):　　Date of Issue (जारी करने की तिथि):　　Place of Issue (जारी करने का स्थान):
(d) Occupation (व्यवसाय):
(e) Address(पता):　NO 822/SD, PS MALVIYA NAGAR, MALVIYA NAGAR, SOUTH, DELHI, INDIA.

7. Details of Known/Suspect/Unknown accused with full particulars(attach separate sheet if necessary)(ज्ञात/ संदिग्ध /अज्ञात अभियुक्त का
का पूरे विवरण सहित वर्णन):

8. Reason for delay in reporting by the complainant/informant (शिकायतकर्ता / सूचनाकर्ता द्वारा रिपोर्ट देरी से दर्ज करने के कारण):
NO DELAY

9. Particulars of the properties stolen/involved (attach separate sheet if necessary):
Sl.No. (क.सं.) Property Type(Description)　　　　　　Est. Value(Rs.)(सूच्य (रु में))

District: SOUTH   P.S: SAKET   Year: 2020   FIR No: 0070   Date: 24/02/2020

10. Total value of property stolen (चोरी हुई सम्पत्ति का कुल मूल्य):

11. Inquest Report / U.D. Case No., if any (मृत्यु समबिन्धत रिपोर्ट / यू.-डी. प्रकरण न., यदि कोई हो):

12. F.I.R. Contents (attach separate sheet, if required)(प्रथम सूचना रिपोर्ट तथ्य):

Statement of Ct. Babulal No. 822/SD PIS No. 28107283 PS Malviya Nagar New Delhi Mobile Number 9610682170 ब्यान किया कि मै थाना मालवीय नगर में बतौर Ct. तैनात हूँ और आज दिनांक 23.02.20 को मै Outer Force एक कम्पनी ITBP के अन्य बाहुबल SHO सहब थाना मालवीय नगर दिल्ली vide DO No.20 B से, गांधी पार्क हौज रानी मालवीय दिल्ली में चल रहे CAA व NRC protest के प्रदर्शनकारियों द्वारा, आज भारत बंद के आह्वान पर गांधी पार्क के आस पास प्रेस एन्क्लेव रोड व मालवीय नगर के अंदर के मुख्य रास्तों पर बाझा जाम करने की आशंका के मद्देनजर कानून व्यवस्था को बनाये के लिए थाना से गांधी पार्क का रवाना हुआ था | जो इसी समय करीब टो ढाई बजे दिन प्रदर्शनकारी भारी संख्या में गांधी पार्क में इकठ्ठा होने लगे जो मंच पर मौजूद इनके नेता जिसमे महिलाये और पुरुष शामिल थे, भीड़ को लाउडस्पीकर पर भाषण टेकर और भीड़ के बीच में घूम घूम कर सड़क पर जाकर बाझा जाम करने के लिए भड़का रहे थे, जिनके नाम बाद में इन्द्राणी उर्फ सानिया, टेविका, पूजा, अनीता, सुनीता, अजरा, मेहरुनमा, सबाना यास्मिन, सबीना तथा हैटर, सलाउद्दीन उर्फ बबलू, आबिद, सलमान, जाहिद, मुन्ना, वासिम गौरी, नड्डू, वकार व रहमान मालूम हुए | जो इसी दौरान सूचना मिलने पर अन्य पुलिस अधिकारी, Outer Force व जिले के अन्य पुलिस स्टाफ और महिला पुलिस स्टाफ के साथ मौका पर पहुंच गए व थे | जो पुलिस अधिकारियों ने इन उच्च प्रदर्शनकारियों को शांतिपूर्वक प्रदर्शन करने और मैक्स हॉस्पिटल के सामने एम्बुलेंस की आवाजाही को ध्यान में रखते हुए, सड़क जाम नहीं करने के बारे में कई बार समझाया था और हालात को देखते हुए एहतियातन पुलिस अधिकारियों ने गांधी पार्क के टोनो तरफ पुलिस barrigade लगाकर इन प्रदर्शनकारियों को सड़क जाम करने के लिए, प्रेस एन्क्लेव रोड की एन्ट्री बंद कर दी थी | जो इसी दौरान वक्त करीब तीन बजे दिन पुलिस की कानून सम्मत हिदायत को टरकाते हुए उपरोक्त व्यक्तियों के भड़काने पर करीब पांच छः सौ महिलाओं और पुरुषों की भीड़ प्रेस एन्क्लेव रोड की तरफ बढ़ने लगी जिन्हें मुश्किल से barrigade की मदद से सड़क पर आने से रोका गया जिस पर उपरोक्त लोगों के इसारे पर यह भीड़ गांधी पार्क से हौज रानी की अंदर ही अंदर होते हुए अचानक से रविदास मंदिर बड़ी मस्जिद व कुम्हार बस्ती से होते हुए प्रेस एन्क्लेव रोड पर आ गयी और मैक्स हॉस्पिटल के बिलकुल सामने सड़क जाम करने लगी जिन्हें महिला पुलिस और अन्य स्टाफ की मदद से मुश्किल से सड़क जाम करने से रोका गया जो इस दौरान उपरोक्त शक्स भीड़ को प्रेस एन्क्लेव रोड पर पुलिस से आगे निकलकर सड़क जाम करने के लिए भड़का रहे थे व इस दौरान पुलिस अधिकारियों भीड़ को मैक्स हॉस्पिटल के इलाज के लिए आयी टेमी व विटेली मरीजों की आवाजाही को देखते हुए, बार बार सड़क जाम नहीं करने और शांति व्यवस्था बनाये रखने के लिए समझा रहे थे | जो उपरोक लोगों के भड़काने पर भीड़ ने प्रेस एन्क्लेव रोड पर कई बार सड़क जाम करने का प्रयास किया लेकिन पुलिस सुरक्षा इंतजामों के कारण अपने मकसद में कामयाब नहीं हो सके और चिड़की गांव main रोड कट पर जाकर धरना प्रदर्शन करने लगी जिससे यहाँ ट्रैफिक में काफी देर तक बाझा उत्पन होती रही जहाँ भी पुलिस अधिकारियों ने इन्हें काफी समझाया | जो इसके बाट भीड़ उपरोक्त व्यक्तियों के भड़काने पर चिड़की गांव से होते हुए कार्नर मार्किट, main मार्किट मालवीय नगर में होते हुए बड़ा गोल चाझा मालवीय नगर पर इकठ्ठा हो गए और main रोड पर धरना प्रदर्शन करते हुए टोबारा कुम्हार बस्ती हौज रानी होते हुए प्रेस एन्क्लेव रोड की तरफ बढ़ने लगे जिन्हें काफी समझाने और सड़क जाम नहीं करने का प्रयास किया गया लेकिन उपरोक्त शक्सों के भड़काने पर यह भीड़ हौज रानी के अंदर से टोबारा बड़ी मस्जिद कट से आगे विभिन्न रास्तों से होते हुए प्रेस एन्क्लेव रोड पर मैक्स हॉस्पिटल के सामने इकठ्ठा होकर भीड़ में शामिल सभी महिलाओं और पुरुष सड़क पर ट्रैफिक जाम करते हुए, गांधी पार्क की तरफ बढ़ने लगे और मैक्स हॉस्पिटल के सामने प्रेस एन्क्लेव रोड पर गांधी पार्क के पास करीब सात बजे शाम सड़क जाम करने के लिए main रोड पर बैठने लगे जिसके कारण सड़क पर मैक्स हॉस्पिटल में पैटन आने जाने वाले मरीजों और सड़क पर मरीजों को ले जा रहे कई वाहनों का रास्ता रुक गया जिन्हें मौका पर मौजूद पुलिस अधिकारियों ने इस बारे में काफी समझाने का प्रयास किया लेकिन वह नहीं माने जो इस दौरान पुलिस अधिकारियों ने loud speaker की मदद से सड़क जाम कर रही भीड़ को कानून व्यवस्था बनाये रखने और सड़क जाम नहीं करने के लिए कई बार समझाया, लेकिन इस दौरान भी उपरोक्त शक्स भीड़ पर लगातार वहीं बैठ जाने और सड़क जाम करने हेतु भड़कावा रहे और अचानक अन्य साथियों की मदद से वहां पर डंडे और पत्थर मंगवाए हाथों में ले लिए व भीड़ के हाथो में दे दिए और जिसके बाट भीड़ में शामिल महिलाओं और पुरुषों ने सड़क पर बैठकर उसे जाम करने की कोशिश की जिस पर महिला पुलिस स्टाफ और अन्य स्टाफ ने उन्हें रोका तो उपरोक्त नामित महिलाओं व पुरुषों ने भीड़ में शामिल अपने अन्य साथियों के साथ महिला पुलिस कर्मियों व अन्य स्टाफ का हमला कर दिया जिससे उन्हें काफी चोटे आई जो प्रदर्शनकारियों के हमले व धक्का मुक्की के कारण ड्यूटी पर तैनात पुलिस कर्मियों को शरीर के कई हिस्सों पर चोटे आई जो 1. W/SI Kamlesh Meena 2. W/HC Usha PS Ambedkar Nagar, 3. W/Ct. Manisha PS Saket, 4. W/Ct. Anju PS Kotla, 5. W/Ct. Shivani PS 6. HC Shiv Kumar PS Malviya Nagar 7. HC Rajesh PS Malviya Nagar 8. Ct. Dharmender PS malviya Nagar 9. Ct. Leelaram PS Malviya Nagar 10. Ct.

District : SOUTH   P.S : SAKET   Year : 2020   FIR No : 0070   Date : 24/02/2020

Rajender Kumar PS Malviya Nagar 11. Ct. Rajender PS Malviya Nagar 12. HC Satender PS Malviya Nagar 13. Ct. Sunil PS Malviya Nagar 14. Ct. Jitender PS Malviya Nagar व अन्य चोटिल पुलिसकर्मियों को बराय डाफ्ट्री अस्पताल भिजवाया गया । जो पर्दर्शनकारियों की हिंसा के कारण कुछ प्रदर्शनकारियों को भी चोटे आई जिनको भी इलाज के लिए हॉस्पिटल भिजवाया गया । जो उपरोक्त घटना की फोटोग्राफी व विडियोग्राफी कराई। तो इसी दौरान उपरोक्त नामित व्यक्तियों ने भीड़ में शामिल अपने अन्य साथियों के साथ मिलकर मेरे ऊपर भी हमला करके मुझे चोट पहुंचाई जिसके बारे में मैंने अपना मैक्स हॉस्पिटल साकेत से अपना इलाज करा लिया है मैंने आपको अपना ध्यान निबाया जो सुन व समझ लिया ठीक है जो उपरोक्त व्यक्तियों और प्रदर्शनकारियों ने मेरे व duty पर तैनात अन्य पुलिसकर्मियों के official duty में बाधा पहुंचाकर और हमारे ऊपर हमला करके हमें चोट पहुंचाई है कानूनी कार्रवाई की जावे। SD English Babu Lal No 822/SD PS Malviya Nagar Attested Sd English SI Ranbir Singh PS Saket 24/02/2020 श्रीमान ड्यूटी ऑफिसर थाना साकेत बकार सरकार निवेदन इस प्रकार है आज मन SI बराय emergency Duty हाजिर थाना साकेत था जो इसी दौरान मुझे MLC No. 2564/20 Of Ct. Babulal No. 822/SD थाना मालवीय नगर बाबत Assault today at around 7.00 pm near press enclave, today evening opposite Max smart hospital Saket Delhi मिलने पर मैं मैक्स स्मार्ट हॉस्पिटल साकेत पहुंचा जहाँ पर Ct. Babulal No. 822/SD थाना मालवीय नगर दिल्ली मिला जिसने दरयाफ्त पर अपना उपरोक्त ब्यान तहरीर कराया है जो इसी दौरान मुझे अभी तक मैक्स स्मार्ट हॉस्पिटल व अन्य हॉस्पिटल से हमें से घायल अन्य पुलिस स्टाफ की भी MLC मिली है जिनका विवरण इस प्रकार है | 1. W/SI Kamlesh Meena 2. W/HC Usha PS Ambedkar Nagar, 3. W/Ct. Manisha PS Saket, 4. W/Ct. Anju PS Kotla, 5. W/Ct. Shivani PS 6. HC Shiv Kumar PS Malviya Nagar 7. HC Rajesh PS Malviya Nagar 8. Ct. Dharmender PS malviya Nagar 9. Ct. Leelaram PS Malviya Nagar 10. Ct. Rajender Kumar PS Malviya Nagar 11. Ct. Rajender PS Malviya Nagar 12. HC Satender PS Malviya Nagar 13. Ct. Sunil PS Malviya Nagar 14. Ct. Jitender PS Malviya Nagar 15. Prem Kumar PS Hauz Khas 16. Satender Kumar PS Hauz Khas 17. Gurpreet Singh PS Hauz Khas 18. Moolchand PS Hauz Khas 19. Arvind PS Hauz Khas 20. Seetaram PS Hauz Khas 21. Deshraj PS Ambedkar Nagar 22. Ct. Jony PS Ambedkar Nagar 23. W/Ct. Rajni PS Saket 24. W/Ct. Sunita PS Saket 25. W/Ct. Seema Cyber Cell South District 26. Ct. Pawan PS Saket जो सभी MLC पर डॉक्टर साहब ने alleged of assault Press Enclave at around 7.00 to 7.30 pm opposite Max Smart Hospital तहरीर कराया है इसी दौरान इस बारे में मन SI ने मौका पर जाकर भी टरयाप्त अमल में लायी जिस पर भीड़ द्वारा सड़क जाम करने से रोकने पर पुलिस पर हमला करके चोट पहुंचाने और सरकारी काम में बाधा डालने के बारे में पता चला जो इस प्रकार ध्यान उपरोक्त से, MLC's से मामला संदर्भित सूरत जुर्म u/s 143/147/148/149/186/353/332/120B/34 IPC का सरजट होना पाया जाता है । निहाजा तहरीर मुकदमा दर्ज कराने के लिए दर पेश है | मुकदमा दर्ज रजिस्टर करके आइन्दा तफ्तीश महुजुमा SHO साहब Insp. Upender Singh ATO PS Saket के की जावे | तारीख व वक्त बकुआ - 23.02.2020 at about 7.00 pm जाय बकुआ - Main Press Enclave Road opposite Max Smart Hospital near Gandhi Park Hauz Rani Saket Delhi तारीख व वक्त येहंगी तहरीर- 24.02.2020 at 1.40 pm SD English SI Ranbir Singh No. 1094/D PS Saket New Delhi 24/02/2020 कार्यवाही पुलिस सूचना पत्र की प्राप्ति पर FIR u/s 143/147/148/149/186/353/332/120B/34 IPC registered Computer करके Copy FIR व मूल लेख की प्रति श्रीमान SHO साहब की आज्ञा से अनुसंधान Insp. Upender साहब की गई जो आगामी कार्यवाही प्रक्रिया में लायेगी अन्य नकल प्रतिया व कागजात डाक द्वारा उच्च अधिकारी की सेवा में प्रस्तुत होगी एक copy FIR MHC(R) को दी गई IHC/DO

13. Action Taken Since the above information reveals commission of offence(s) u/s as mentioned at Item No. 2:
(की गयी कार्यवाही: चूंकि उपरोक्त जानकारी से पता चलता है कि किया गया अपराध मद सं.2 में उल्लेख धारा के तहत है):

   (i) Registered the case and took up the Investigation: OR (या)
   (प्रकरण दर्ज किया गया और जांच के लिए लिया गया):

   (ii) Directed [Name of the I.O.](जांच अधिकारी का नाम): UPENDRA KUMAR SINGH   Rank (पद): I (INSPECTOR)

   No.(सं.): 16970052   to take up the investigation (को जांच अपने पास में लेने के लिए निर्देश दिया गया) OR(या)

   (iii) Refused investigation due to(जांच के लिए):   OR (के कारण इंकार किया वा)

   (iv) Transferred to P.S(name)(थाना):   District(जिला):
   on point of jurisdiction (को क्षेत्राधिकार के कारण हस्तांतरित)

F.I.R read over to the complainant/informant,admitted to be correctly recorded and a copy given to the complainant/informant, free of cost : (शिकायतकर्ता / सूचनाकर्ता को प्राथिमिकी पढ़ कर सुनाई गयी, सही दर्ज हुई माना और एक कॉपी निशुल्क शिकायतकर्ता को दी गयी) :

R.O.A.C.(आर.ओ.ए.सी.):

14. Signature / Thumb Impression of the Complainant / Informant: **Signature of Officer**
(शिकायतकर्ता / सूचनाकर्ता के हस्ताक्षर / अंगूठे का निशान):   Name(नाम): RAJENDER KUMAR
     Rank (पद): HC (HEAD CONSTABLE)
     No.(सं.): 28960010

15. Date and Time of despatch to the court:
(अदालत में प्रेषण की दिनांक और समय):

FIRST INFORMATION REPORT

(Under Section 154 Cr P C)

(धारा 154 दं प्रक्रिया संहिता के तहत)

1. District (जिला) NORTH EAST   P S (थाना) KARAWAL NAGAR   Year(वर्ष) 2020   FIR No(प्र.सू.रि. सं.) 16653   Date 25-03-2020

2. Act(s)(अधिनियम)   Section(s)(धारा(एँ))
    IPC 1860   147/148/149/336/427/307
    - PREVENTION OF DAMAGE TO   3/4
    PUBLIC PROPERTY ACT 1984

3. Occurrence of Offence (अपराध की घटना)
   (a)Day(दिन)   MONDAY   Date From(दिनांक से)   24/02/2020   Date To(दिनांक तक):   24/02/2020
   Time Period (समय अवधि)   Time From (समय से):   14 30 Hrs   Time To (समय तक) ,   14 30 Hrs
   (b)Information received at P S (सूचना थाना पहुँचने का समय और तारीख)   Date(दिनांक): 25/02/2020   Time (समय) 17 55 Hrs
   (c)General Diary Reference (दैनिकी प्रविष्टि संदर्भ):   Entry No.(प्रविष्टि सं.) 022A   Date/Time(दिनांक/समय) 25/02/2020 18 05

4. Type of Information (सूचना का प्रकार): Written

5. Place of Occurrence (घटनास्थल)
   (a) Direction and Distance from P S (थाना से दूरी और दिशा), EAST 2 Km(s)   Beat No(बीट सं.) , 03
   (b) Address(पता): ROAD PAR SAREAAM SHIV VIHAR TIRAHA, KARAWAL NAGAR
   (c) In case, Outside the limit of the Police Station (यदि थाना सीमा से बाहर हो):
     Name of P S (थाना का नाम): KARAWAL NAGAR   District(जिला): NORTH EAST(UD)

6. Complainant / Informant (शिकायतकर्ता/सूचनाकर्ता)
   (a)Name(नाम): PATE KUMAR
   (b)Date/Year of Birth (जन्म तिथि/वर्ष), 01/06/1986   Nationality (राष्ट्रीयता)   INDIA
   (c)Passport No (पासपोर्ट सं.):   Date of Issue (जारी करने की तिथि):   Place of Issue (जारी करने का स्थान)
   (d)Occupation (व्यवसाय)
   (e)Address(पता): DELHI, OUTER DISTRICT, DELHI, INDIA, 9015671593

7. Details of Known/Suspect/Unknown accused with full particulars(attach separate sheet if necessary)(ज्ञात/शंकित/अज्ञात अभियुक्त का पूरा विवरण संलग्न करें)

8. Reason for delay in reporting by the complainant/informant (शिकायतकर्ता / सूचनाकर्ता द्वारा रिपोर्ट देने में हुई देरी के कारण).
   NO DELAY

9. Particulars of the properties stolen/involved (attach separate sheet if necessary)
   Sl No (क्र.सं.) Property Type(Description)   Est Value(Rs.) (मूल्य (रु.में))

10. Total value of property stolen (चोरी हुई सम्पत्ति का कुल मूल्य):

11. Inquest Report / U.D Case No., if any [मृत्यु समीक्षा रिपोर्ट / यू.डी. प्रकरण न., यदि कोई हो]:

12. F.I.R. Contents [attach separate sheet, if required/इसके पृथक रिपोर्ट लगाए]:

The statement s of HC Patil No 3283/NE P.S KARAWAL NAGAR DELHI ब्यान किया कि मैं उपरा उपरोक्त नगर हिo कवीं HC मिलता हूं तथा Date- 24/02/20 को citizensip amendmet ACT (CAA)का विरोध को देखने हुए सिख विहार तिराहे पर पुलिस इंतजाम लगाया गया था जो मैं अन्य पुलिस स्टाफ HC RANVEER NO 517/NE . HC SHAFEEQ No 1843/NE . Ct Suni No 2836/NE . Ct Tejpal no 1287/NE . Ct Subham no 1123/NE. Ct santosh 3402/Ne, Ct Ajay No 2712/NE, Ct Anuj No 1019/NE . Ct Ravinder No 2763/NE, Ct Ashok No 1437/NE के साथ वहां करीब 2 30 बजे ट्रेफिक मौजूद था जो वहां पर काफी लोग CAA के विरोधक में यहां इक्ठ्ठे थे यह प्रदर्शन कर रहे थे जो काफी लोग यहां चल रही थी जिसमें ज्यादातर मुस्लिम समुदाय के लोग थे जो उनके नारे लगाने से वहां इलाके में तनाव उत्पन्न पैदा हो रहा था जो मैने जाने के फोन का सिविलीन अफसरों को मौका पर पहुंचने के लिये थाने में बतलाया जो सूचना पर जो पर SHO Sanjeev Kumar साहब आये जिन्होंने वहां मौजूद भीड़ को काफी समझाने कि कोशिश कि लेकिन वहां भीड़ के लोग काफी उग्र थे और हाथों में डंडा व पत्थर मुसलमानावाद कि तरफ से अक्सर सिख विहार तिराहे पर मस्टिर कि तरफ बढ रहे थे तथा मरने मारने पर इतारू थे जो SHO साहब ने प्रोटेशन अफिसरो को द्वारा से चेतावनी दी तथा भीड़ को शान्त करने की कोशिस की व समझाया कि अगर आप विधि पूर्वक चेतावनी का पालन नही करोगे तो आप पर कानूनी कार्यवाही की जायेगी तो भीड़ में एक मत होकर वहां पर मौजूद दूसरे समुदाय के लोग पर पथराव शुरू दिया व पथराव करने लगे व इंटें बरसाने लगे जो पत्थर शुरू दिया व पथराव चलने लगे व इंटें बरसाने लगे जो पत्थर मारने से कुछ लोग घायल हो गये इसी दौरान भीड़ को गोलियां चलाने आवाज़ आयी जो मौका पर Add Force आने के बाद का मुश्किल हालात पर काबू पाया गया इसके बाद उक्त उग्र टाइडैने में अलग-अलग जगह पर ज्वलन टुकड़ी में नोट फोड़ व आग लगाकर आगजनी की तथा सिख विहार चौक पर खड़ी fire सर्विस की गाड़ी में आग लगा दी तथा सिख विहार में कहीं जगह टुकड़ो में तोड़ फोड़ कर आग लगा दी इस पत्थर बारी व गोली चलाने से काफी लोग घायल हो गये जो उक्त प्रोटेनशरियो ने गैरकानूनी तरीके से ईकट्ठा होकर डंडे व पत्थर व अश्रफ्त में खड़ी गाड़ी को नोट पहुंचाई व एक टुकर पर जान लेवा हमला किया तथा वहां पर खड़ी गाड़ियो में दूसरे समुदाय की टुकड़ो में आग लगाकर काफी पब्लिक प्रॉपर्टी को छति पहुंचाई है इन टाइडियों में से कुछ लोग को सामने आने का पहचान सकता हूं इन टाइडियों के खिलाफ कानूनी कार्यवाही की जाये। ब्यान सुन लिया ठीक है SD English HC Patil Attested ASI RAKAM SINGH PS KARAWAL NAFGAR Delhi Dt 25/02/20 श्रीमान DO साहब थाना कायम नगर हिo सरकारी काम में अनुरोध है कि मैं ASI मय हमराही Ct सुभम no 1123/NE DD NO 45A DT 24/02/20मैंने वर घटना स्थान पर पहुंचा या जहां पर काफी नोह इकट्ठा होकर तोड़ फोड़ कर तोड़ फोड़ व आगजनी कर रहे थे जो मैं भी अन्य staff के साथ काबू करने का प्रयास करता रहा जो इसी टोमेन DD No 134A मिलने पर मय हमराही Ct उपरोक्त G T B. आश्वस्त हिo 7 PM पहुंचा था जहां पर MLC NO D-9 जनाब सीरियस s/o फेरू R/o फेस- 9 धर्मी -3 सिख विहार हिo व MLC NO D-7 भी हासिल की जिसपर डाक्टर साहब ने A/HO fee Arm enjury लिखा था जो इसी टोसे पता चला कि घटना में कुछ लोग घायल हो हम इस अश्वस्ताल व अन्य अस्पतालों में गये हैं जिसपर वह ASI मय हमराही Ct उपरोक्त था एण्ड आर्म इन्जूरी जनने मौका पर पहुंचा जो उस समय टागेई अस्म -2 स्थानो पर तोड़ फोड़ व आगजनी कर रहे थे कोई अन्य चश्मदीद गवाह मौका पर नही मिला मन ASI मय हमराही staff तथा एण्ड आर्म इन्जूरी उसके हाजिर ज्ञाता पहुंचा जहां पर MLC पर्टिन NO 3283/NE ने अपना ब्यान दंड कराया ब्यान उपरोक्त मे MLC से व PCR CALL है व हल्फत मौका से सामना जुर्म U/S 147/148/149/336/427/307 IPC व 3/4 DP DP Act का होना पाया जाता है निहातम एक लिखित प्रलेख तैयार करके थाने में प्रस्तुत है मु. दर्ज रेजि० करके मु. संख्या से अवगत कराया जाये मैं ASI नुरुद्दम की तहरीर में ध्यान है घटना कि तारीख व समय DT 24/2/20AT 2.30PM घटना स्थान – सिख विहार तिराहा सर्व आम ज्वलन नगर हिo संख्या भंवने कि नागरिक व समय DT 25/2/20 AT 5.55PM पुलिस कार्यवाही स्थम HC/DO की ASI RALKAM SINGH ने हिन्दी में लिखित एक प्रलेख मुख्तसर पंजीकरण हेतु स्थम आफसर मुख HC/DO की पहल्त कि प्रबंध के जिनपर स्थम HC/Do ने थेम FIR No 53/20 U/S 147/148/149/336/427/307 IPC & 3/4 DP.DP ACT रजिस्टर करके व CCIIHS SAMP में Computerized FIR करके original प्रलेख तथा Computerized FIR Copy Investigation के लिए By order SHO साहब Asi RAKAM SINGH साहब को दी गयी जो आगे की Investigation करेंगे अन्य निमिनिय डाक के टवका यह प्रतिकलियो के नाम भिजवाये जायेंगे सूचना पंजीकृत की गई

13 Action Taken: Since the above information reveals commission of offence(s) u/s as mentioned at Item No. 2

(i) Registered the case and took up the investigation:

(ii) Directed (Name of the I.O.) NARAM SINGH   Rank (पद) ASST S(ASSISTANT SUB-INSPECTOR)

No. (सं.) 23531495   to take up the investigation (को अन्वेषण करने के लिए निर्देश दिया गया) OR (या)

(iii) Refused investigation due to (जांच के लिए)

(iv) Transferred to P.S.(name/जिला)   District/(जिला)

on point of jurisdiction (को क्षेत्राधिकार के कारण हस्तांतरित)

F.I.R. read over to the complainant/informant, admitted to be correctly recorded and a copy given to the complainant/informant, free of cost

R.O.A.C. (आर.ओ.ए.सी.)

14 Signature / Thumb Impression of the Complainant / Informant

Signature of Officer

Name(नाम) BIPIN KUMAR YADAV

Rank (पद) HC (HEAD CONSTABLE)

No.(सं.) 28/89321

15 Day and Time of dispatch to the court

FIRST INFORMATION REPORT
(Under Section 154 Cr.P.C.)

(धारा 154 दंड प्रकिया संहिता के तहत)

1. District (जिला):NORTH EAST   P.S.(थाना): DAYAL PUR   Year(वर्ष): 2020   FIR No(प्र.सू.रि.सं.):0060   Date :25/02/2020

2. Act(s)(अधिनियम):
   - IPC 1860   Section(s)(धारा(एँ):
   - PREV. OF DAMAGE TO PUBLIC PROPERTY ACT. 3/4   186/353/332/323/147/148/149/336/427/307/302
     1984

3. Occurrence of Offence (अपराध की घटना):
   (a)Day(दिन):   INTERVENING DAY   Date From(दिनांक से):   24/02/2020   Date To(दिनांक तक):   25/02/2020
   Time Period (समय अवधि):   Time From (समय से):   13:00 hrs   Time To (समय तक):   16:00 hrs
   (b)Information received at P.S.(थाना पर सूचना प्राप्त हुई):   Date(दिनांक): 25/02/2020   Time (समय): 16:06 hrs
   (c)General Diary Reference (रोजनामचा संदर्भ):   Entry No.(प्रविष्टि सं.): 14SA   Date/Time(दिनांक/समय): 25/02/2020 16:06

4. Type of Information (सूचना का प्रकार): Written

5. Place of Occurrence (घटनास्थान):
   (a) Direction and Distance from P.S (थाना से दूरी और दिशा): N/A , 02 Km(s)   Beat No(बीट सं.) : 02
   (b) Address(पता): MAIN ROAD WAZIRABAD ROAD ,NEAR CHAND BAGH DELHI
   (c) In case, Outside the limit of the Police Station (यदि, थाना सीमा के बाहर है):
   Name of P.S(थाना का नाम):   District(जिला):

6. Complainant / Informant (शिकायतकर्ता/सूचनाकर्ता):
   (a)Name(नाम): CT SUNIL
   (b)Date/Year of Birth (जन्म तिथि /वर्ष):   Nationality (राष्ट्रीयता):   INDIA
   (c)Passport No.(पासपोर्ट सं.):   Date of Issue (जारी करने की तिथि):   Place of Issue (जारी करने का स्थान):
   (d)Occupation (व्यवसाय):
   (e)Address(पता): PS DAYALPUR, DAYAL PUR, NORTH EAST, DELHI, INDIA,

7. Details of Known/Suspect/Unknown accused with full particulars(attach separate sheet if necessary)(ज्ञात/संदिग्ध /अज्ञात अभियुक्त का का पूरे विवरण सहित वर्णन):

8. Reason for delay in reporting by the complainant/informant (शिकायतकर्ता / सूचनाकर्ता द्वारा रिपोर्ट देरी से दर्ज कराने के कारण):
   NO DELAY

9. Particulars of the properties stolen/involved (attach separate sheet if necessary):
   Sl.No. (क्र.सं.) Property Type(Description)   Est. Value(Rs.)(अनुमानित मूल्य (रु में))

District: NORTH EAST   P.S. DAYAL PUR   Year: 2020   FIR No. 60/6   Date: 25/02/20

10. Total value of property stolen (चोरी हुई सामग्री का कुल मूल्य):

11. Inquest Report / U.D. Case No., if any (शुनतु संबंधित रिपोर्ट / यू.डी. प्रकरण न., यदि कोई हो):

12. F.I.R. Contents (attach separate sheet, if required)(प्रथम सूचना रिपोर्ट तथ्य):

ब्यान आजने Ct Sunil Kumar, No. 2907/NE, PIS No. 28105705, PS Dayalpur, Delhi. Age-43 Years, M.No. 9560361661, ब्यान किया कि मैं दिल्ली पुलिस में बतौर सिपाही तैनात हूं और इन दिनों मेरी ड्यूटि PS Dayalpur, District North-East में चल रही है जो मे चौट बाग चौट में कार्यरत हूं। जो Citizen Ship Amendment Act (CAA) के विरोध में मुस्लिम समुदाय के लोग पिछले करीब 1.5 महीने से कानूनी चौक से लोगो गोल बझर कि तरफ जाने वाली वजीराबाद रोड पर चौट बाग नजदीक 25 फुट्टा रोड सर्विस रोड पर प्रदर्शन चल रहे थे । जो मेरी Law & Order Arrangement Duty वहीं पर थाने के अन्य स्टाफ के साथ लगी थी । और वही पर ACP Gokulpuri, Shri Anuj Kumar साहब व आपके साथ अन्य स्टाफ जिसमे HC Giri Chand, No. 840/NE, Ct Mahavir No. 3247/NE, Ct. Jitender No. 1246/NE, HC Ratan Lal No. 1282/NE, HC Narender No. 1187/NE, HC Brijesh, W/HC Savitri No. 454/NE & W/HC Sonia No. 1549/NE. भी मौजूद थे । जो इसके अलावा Sahadara District के DCP Amit Kumar Sharma साहब भी अपने स्टाफ के साथ मौजूद थे। जो पहले प्रदर्शनकारी सर्विस रोड पर थे लेकिन दिन में लगभग 1 बजे तमाम प्रदर्शनकारी सर्विस रोड से वजीराबाद Main Road की तरफ आने लगे जो मौके पर मौजूद Senior officers ने उन्हे काफी मना किया और भीड़ मे प्रदर्शनकारी को काफी समझाने की कोशिश की लेकिन भीड़ के लोग काफी उग्र थे । और हाथो मे डंडे, Base Ball Stick, Iron Road व पत्थर लिए मरने मारने पर उतारू थे । जो ACP Gokulpuri साहब व DCP Shahdara साहब ने प्रदर्शनकारियो को टोबारा चेतावनी दी और उन्हे सरकारी गाड़ी मे लगे Loud Hailer से चेतावनी दी की अगर आप विधि पूर्वक चेतावनी का पालन नहीं करेंगे तो आप पर कानूनी कार्यवाही की जायेगी । जो भीड़ मे छड़े छड़े लोगो ने एक मत होकर पुलिस पार्टी पर पथराव शुरू कर दिया व उनके पास पहले से टैंट मे छुपाकर रखे गये डंडे, Base Ball, Iron Road आदि से पुलिस व राह चलते लोगो को मारने पीटने लगे जो पत्थर लगाने से मेरी Right Side Elbow & Right Hand मे चोट आई है । जो प्रदर्शनकारियो की संख्या इतनी ज्यादा थी की उन्होने पुलिस स्टाफ के लोगो से Gas Gole छीन लिए व पुलिस की भी लाठिया छीन कर उनसे प्रहार करने लगे जो मेरे सामने ही उस भीड़ मे जिसमे महिलाए भी थी न ने ACP Gokulpuri उनके स्टाफ HC Ratan Lal व DCP Shahdara Amit Kumar Sharma साहब के ऊपर भी पथराव करके डंडे आदि से मारना शुरू कर दिया । जिससे ACP, DCP व HC Ratan Lal वही गिर गए और उनके ऊपर भारी पथराव होने से उनके सिर फट गये जिनसे खून बहने लगा और गंभीर चोट आई जो मैं Additional Force आने के बाद भीड़ को काबू किया गया । व दंगाइयो को भगाया गया और घायलो को हॉस्पिटल भेजा गया और बाद मे, मैने Panchsheeal Hospital Yamuna Vihar, Delhi. मे अपना इलाज कराया । जो बाद मे मुझे पता चला की ACP Gokulpuri साहब के ऑफिस मे तैनात HC Ratan Lal की सिर मे गंभीर चोट लगने से मौत हो गयी है व ACP Gokulpuri साहब व DCP Shahdara Amit Sharma साहब को भी गंभीर चोटे आई है । जो कुछ हम पुलिस वालो और पब्लिक के लोगो को भी चोटे आई है जो प्रदर्शनकारियो ने गैर कानूनी तरीके से इकट्ठा होकर डंडे, Base Ball Bat, Iron Road और पत्थरो से लेस होकर पुलिस स्टाफ पर जान लेवा हमला किया है जिसमे HC Ratan Lal की मृत्यु हो गयी है । तथा दंगा फसाद किया है व पुलिस बल से डंडे व गैस गोले छीने है तथा DCP Shahdara साहब की सरकारी गाड़ी व अन्य पुलिस वालो के निजी वाहनो को आग के हवाले करके सरकारी व गैर सरकारी सम्पत्ति को क्षति पहुचाई है । इन दंगाइयो के खिलाफ कानूनी कार्यवाही की जाये । जो इस हादसे के वक बुछ पब्लिक के लोग Private Mobile से Video भी बना रहे थे जो मैं उस भीड़ के लोगो को सामने आने पर पहचान सकता हूं । जो आपने मेरा ब्यान लिखा पढ़ लिया ठीक है । Sd English Ct Sunil No. 2907/NE, Attested ASI Heera Lal No. 770/NE, PS Dayalpur, श्रीमान DO साहब थाना Dayalpur, Delhi. निवेदन है कि दिनांक 24/02/2020 को DD No. 52A, जिसने पर मन ASI मय Ct Ankit No. 1562/NE, GTB Hospital पहुंचा जहां पर MLC No. B-8537/02/2020. आजने HC Ratan Lal S/o Brij Mohan R/o Barrack No. 07, 3rd Floor, PS Krishana Nagar, Delhi. Age-53 Years, हाजिल की जिसपर Doctor साहब ने मजरूब को Brought Dead At 2:13 PM on 24/02/2020 तहरीर फरमाया व Dead Body, GTB Hospital Mortuary भिजवाई गयी जो मैने हालत SHO साहब को बतलायो । इसके बाद DD No. 59A की इत्तला DO/PS Dayalpur से मिलने पर मैं स्टाफ के साथ Panchsheel Hospital Yamuna Vihar पहुंचा था जहां पर MLC No. 10303/2020 आजने Ct Sunil Kumar, PS Dayalpur, Age-43 Years हाजिल की जिसपर डॉक्टर साहब ने Nature of Injury Simple तथा पब्लिक Violence (Stone Pelting) at Chand Bagh Wazirabad Road on 24/02/2020 at 01: 20 PM तहरीर फरमाया । व Hospital मे मजरूब व अन्य कोई चसमदीद गवाह नही मिला । मैं ASI हमराही स्टाफ के साथ थाना पहुंचा था जहां पर Ct सुनील उपरोक मिला व अपना ब्यान उपरोक तहरीर कराया जो ब्यान उपरोक से MLC की Injuries से व हालात से अपराध U/s 186/353/332/323/147/148/149/336/427/307/302 IPC व 3/4 PDPP Act का होना पाया

2

Destt.: NORTHEAST	P.S.: DAYALPUR	Year: 2020	FIR No: 0060	Date: 25/02/2020

गया है निहाजा एक हिन्दी लेख तैयार किया गया व DO PS Dayalpur को मुकदमा दर्ज करने के लिए पेश किया जो मुकदमा दर्ज करके मुकदमा की तफ्तीश किसी Insp. साहब के हवाले की जाए। मैं ASI स्टाफ के साथ Law & order Duty का रखना होता हूं। तारीख व वक्त चकुआ:- 24/02/2020 at around 1:00 PM, जगह वकुआ:- Main Wazirabad Road, Near Chand Bagh, Delhi, तारीख व वक्त पेशगी तहरीर:- 25/02/2020 at 16:00 HRS पुलिस कार्यवाही एक हिन्दी लिखित लेख ASI Heeralal No.770/NE साहब द्वारा HC/DO साहब को मिला जो लेख मिलने पर मुकदमा नं 60/2020 U/S 186/353/332/323/147/148/149/336/427/307/302 IPC व 3/4 PDPP Act दर्ज करके CCTNS Operator द्वारा Computer में Feed कराकर असली लेख के साथ FIR की Computerized Copy हवाले ATO INSP. HUKAM SINGH साहब के की जा रही है। जो बाहुबम जनाब SHO साहब आईन्दा तफ्तीश अमल में लावेंगे। अन्य नकल प्रतिलिपियां स्पेशल मैसेन्जर द्वारा वरिष्ठ अधिकारियों को भिजवायी जा रही है। Submitted by HC/DO.

13.Action Taken Since the above information reveals commission of offence(s) u/s as mentioned at item No. 2:
(की गयी कार्यवाही: चूंकि उपरोक्त जानकारी से पता चलता है कि किया गया अपराध मद सं.2.में उल्लेख धारा के तहत है):

                                                           OR (या)

(i)Registered the case and took up the Investigation:
- (फसला दर्ज किया गया और जांच के लिए लिया गया):

(ii) Directed (Name of the I.O.)(जांच अधिकारी का नाम): HUKAM SINGH

                                                  Rank (पद):
                                                  I (INSPECTOR)

No.(सं.): 16040045   to take up the investigation (जो जांच आगमे चाहे में लेने के लिए निर्देश दिया गया) OR(या)

(iii)Refused investigation due to(जांच के लिए):   OR (के कारण इंकार किया गया)

(iv) Transferred to P.S(name)(थाना):   District(जिला):
on point of jurisdiction (जो क्षेत्राधिकार के कारण हस्तांतरित):

F.I.R read over to the complainant/informant,admitted to be correctly recorded and a copy given to the complainant/informant, free of cost : (शिकायतकर्ता / सूचनाकर्ता को शब्दशिश पढ़ कर सुनाई गयी, सही दर्ज हुई माना और एक कॉपी निःशुल्क शिकायतकर्ता को दी गयी) :

R.O.A.C.(आर.ओ.ए.सी.):

14.Signature / Thumb Impression
of the Complainant / Informant:
(शिकायतकर्ता / सूचनाकर्ता के हस्ताक्षर / अंगूठे का निशान):

                                  Signature of Officer
                                  Name(नाम): KULDEEP UJJAWAL
                                  Rank (पद): HC (HEAD CONSTABLE)
                                  No.(सं.): 28101830

15.Date and Time of despatch to the court:
(अदालत में प्रेषण की दिनांक और समय):

FIRST INFORMATION REPORT
(Under Section 154 Cr.P.C.)

(धारा 154 दंड प्रक्रिया संहिता के तहत)

1. District (जिला):NORTH EAST   P.S.(थाना): DAYAL PUR   Year(वर्ष): 2020   FIR No(प्र.सू.रि.सं.):0075   Date : 28/02/2020

2. Act(s)(अधिनियम):   Section(s)(धारा(एं)):
   - IPC 1860   147/148/149/436/302/120B/34

3. Occurrence of Offence (अपराध की घटना):
   (a)Day(दिन):   MONDAY   Date From(दिनांक से): 24/02/2020   Date To(दिनांक तक):   24/02/2020
   Time Period (समय अवधि):   Time From (समय में): 00:00 hrs   Time To (समय तक):   00:00 hrs
   (b)Information received at P.S.(थाना जहां सूचना प्राप्त हुई):   Date(दिनांक): 28/02/2020   Time (समय): 01:20 hrs
   (c)General Diary Reference (रोजनामचा संदर्भ):   Entry No.(प्रविष्टि सं.): 008A   Date/Time(दिनांक/समय): 28/02/2020 01:27

4. Type of Information (सूचना का प्रकार):   Written

5. Place of Occurrence (घटनास्थल):
   (a) Direction and Distance from P.S (थाना से दूरी और दिशा): NORTH-WEST , 3 Km(s)   Beat No(बीट सं.) : 08
   (b) Address(पता): GALI NO 01, ,PAL DAIRY WALI GALI ,KE SAMNE MAHALAXMI ENCLAVE, KARAWAL NAGAR DELHI-94
   (c) In case, Outside the limit of the Police Station (यदि थाना सीमा के बाहर है):
   Name of P.S(थाना का नाम):   District(जिला):

6. Complainant / Informant (शिकायतकर्ता/सूचनाकर्ता):
   (a)Name(नाम): HEMRAJ RAJ SINGH
   (b)Date/Year of Birth (जन्म तिथि/वर्ष): 05/12/1970   Nationality (राष्ट्रीयता):   INDIA
   (c)Passport No.(पासपोर्ट सं.):   Date of Issue (जारी करने की तिथि):   Place of Issue (जारी करने का स्थान):
   (d)Occupation (व्यवसाय):
   (e)Address(पता): HARSHVIHAR, WELCOME, NORTH EAST, DELHI, INDIA, 9818541637,

7. Details of Known/Suspect/Unknown accused with full particulars(attach separate sheet if necessary)(ज्ञात/संदिग्ध /अज्ञात अभियुक्त का का पूरे विवरण सहित वर्णन):

8. Reason for delay in reporting by the complainant/informant (शिकायतकर्ता / सूचनाकर्ता द्वारा रिपोर्ट देरी से दर्ज कराने के कारण):
   NO DELAY

9. Particulars of the properties stolen/involved (attach separate sheet if necessary):
   Sl.No. (क्र.सं.) Property Type(Description)   Est. Value(Rs.)(मूल्य (रु में))

10. Total value of property stolen (चोरी हुई सम्पत्ति का कुल मूल्य):

11. Inquest Report / U.D. Case No.. if any (मृत्यु कयी/प्रा रिपोर्ट / यू.डी. प्रकरण न., यदि कोई हो):

District : NORTH EAST   P.S. DAYAL PUR   Year: 2020   FIR No. 075   Date 24/02/2020

12.F.I.R. Contents (attach separate sheet, if required)(प्रथम सूचना रिपोर्ट तत्व):

DD NO.40B DATED 24/02/2020, PS DAYALPUR, DELHI DO द्वारा आमद एमएलसी जीटीबी हॉस्पिटल BY PHONE समय 11:15 बजे रात दर्ज है कि कॉन्स्टेबल अशोक 2124/SHD ने बजरिये टेलीफोन इत्तला दी है कि राहुल सोलंकी S/O धीर सिंह सोलंकी R/O मकान नंबर 174 गली नंबर 5 बाबू नगर दिल्ली उम्र 26 साल को शिव मंदिर तिराहे पर गोली लगने से CT अनिल PS LONI ने GTB हॉस्पिटल में भर्ती कराया है जो डॉक्टर साहब ने मृत घोषित कर दिया है जिसकी एमएलसी नंबर BD-542/02/2020 है हस्त आमद टेलीफोन इत्तला दम रोजनामचा की गयी व इस्तला IO ASI HEMRAJ SINGH NO. 405/NE बराये मुनासिब कार्यवाही की गई । बदस्तूर HC/DO ASI RAMA PRAKASH NO.149/NE PS DAYALPUR, DELHI-94. NOTE-TRUE COPY बीमान DO साहब थाना दयालपुर दिल्ली बखत सरकार निवेदन है की मन ASI को MLC इत्तला DD NO.40-B, DATED 24/02/2020 मिलने पर मन ASI GTB HOSPITAL पहुंचा MLC NO.BD/542/02/2020 आजने राहुल सोलंकी S/O धीर सिंह सोलंकी R/O मकान नंबर 174 गली नंबर 5 बाबू नगर दिल्ली उम्र 26 साल हासिल की व बता चला की राहुल सोलंकी की DEAD BODY को GTB HOSPITAL की MOURTHARY में PRESERVE किया जा चूका है MLC पर DR साहब ने PATIENT BROUGHT TO MAIN CASUELTY IN UNCONSSIOUS AND UNRESPONSIVE STATE A/H/O PATIENT FOUND LYING AT EVNAN AT AROUND 09 PM ON 24/02/2020 AS HISTORY OF GUNSHOOT AS STATED BY BROUGHT BY तहरीर दर्जमाया है जो मामला DD ENTRY की तहरीक्त से मुलाहिजा DEAD BODY से MLC से LOCAL तहरीक्त से मालूम हुआ की CAA के विरोधी प्रदर्शन के दंगों के दौरान जख्मी होकर मृत्यु हुई है जो मामला सरेदस्त फौत जुर्म U/S 147/148/149/436/302/120B/34 IPC फ़त सरदस्त होना पाया जाता है । तहरीर हज़ा CAA के विरोधी प्रदर्शन के दंगों की ड्यूटी में व्यस्त के कारण कार्यवाही कयम अमल में लायी जा रही है तहरीर हज़ा बर्गब कायमी मुक़द्दमा दर्ज रजिस्टर करके आइन्दा तफ्तीश INSPECTOR HUKAM SINGH साहब के हवाले की जावे मन ASI मशरूफ व तफ्तीश हूं । तारीख वक्त वकूआ :- 24/02/20 TIME NOT KNOWN जाये वकूआ :- G. NO.01, शाम हेरी वाली गली के सामने महालक्ष्मी एन्क्लेव करवाल नगर, दिल्ली -94, तारीख वक्त टेलेग्री तहरीर :-29 /02/2020 AT-1:20am कार्यवाही पुलिस अदम थाना एक हिन्दी लिखित लेखनुसार ASI HEMRAJ NO-405/NE ने HC/DO साहब को लेख पेश किया जो लेख की पैरवी पर मु० न० 75/2020 U/S 147/148/149/436/302/120B/34 IPC दर्ज करके CCTNS OPERATOR द्वारा COMPUTER में FEED कराकर असली लेख के साथ FIR की Computerized Copy INSP. HUKAM SINGH साहब को भिजवायी जा रही है। जो आईन्दा तफ्तीश अमल में लायेंगे। अन्य नकल प्रतिलिपियां डाक द्वारा वरिष्ठ उच्च अधिकारियों को भिजवायी जायेंगे SUBMITTED BY HC/DO.

13.Action Taken: Since the above Information reveals commission of offence(s) u/s as mentioned at item No. 2:

(की गयी कार्यवाही: चूंकि उपरोक्त जानकारी से पता चलता है कि किया गया अपराध मद सं.2.में इस्तेमाल धारा के तहत है):

     OR (या)

(i)Registered the case and took up the Investigation:

(प्रकरण दर्ज किया गया और जांच के लिए लिया गया):

(ii)Directed (Name of the I.O.)(जांच अधिकारी का नाम): HUKAM SINGH   Rank (पद): I (INSPECTOR)

No(नं.): 16040045   to take up the investigation (को जांच आगे बढ़ाने के लिए निर्देश दिया गया) OR(या)

(iii)Refused Investigation due to(जांच के लिए):   OR (के कारण इंकार किया गया)

(iv)Transferred to P.S(name)(थाना):   District(जिला):

on point of jurisdiction (क्षेत्राधिकार के कारण हस्तांतरित)

F.I.R read over to the complainant/informant, admitted to be correctly recorded and a copy given to the complainant/informant, free of cost : (शिकायतकर्ता / सूचनाकर्ता को प्राथमिकी पढ़ कर सुनाई गयी, सही दर्ज हुई माना और एक प्रति निःशुल्क शिकायतकर्ता को दी गयी) :

R.O.A.C.(आर.ओ.ए.सी.):

14.Signature / Thumb Impression   Signature of Officer

of the Complainant / Informant:

(शिकायतकर्ता / सूचनाकर्ता के हस्ताक्षर / अंगूठे का निशान):   Name(नाम): RAKESH KUMAR

Rank (पद): HC (HEAD CONSTABLE)

No.(नं.): 28900490

15.Date and Time of despatch to the court:

(अदालत में रेषण की तिथि और समय):

FIRST INFORMATION REPORT
(Under Section 154 Cr.P.C.)

(धारा 154 दं.प्र.सं. के तहत)

1. District (जिला) NORTH EAST   P.S.(थाना): KHAJURI KHAS   Year(वर्ष) 2020   FIR No(प्र.सू.रि.सं.):0122   Date : 28/02/2020

2. Act(s)(अधिनियम):   Section(s)(धारा(एँ)):
   - IPC 1860   147/148/149/427/04
   - PREV. OF DAMAGE TO PUBLIC PROPERTY ACT. 3/4
     1984

3. Occurrence of Offence (अपराध की घटना):
   (a) Day(दिन):   MONDAY   Date From(दिनांक से): 24/02/2020   Date To(दिनांक तक):   24/02/2020
      Time Period (समय अवधि):   Time From (समय से):   14:30 hrs   Time To (समय तक):   14:30 hrs
   (b)Information received at P.S.(थाना पहुँ सूचना प्राप्त हुई):   Date(दिनांक): 28/02/2020   Time (समय): 17:55 hrs
   (c)General Diary Reference (रोजनामचा संदर्भ):   Entry No.(प्रविष्टि सं.): 041A   Date/Time(दिनांक/समय):28/02/2020 18:02

4. Type of Information (सूचना का प्रकार): Written

5. Place of Occurrence (घटनास्थल):
   (a) Direction and Distance from P.S (थाना से दूरी और दिशा): EAST , 2 Km(s)   Beat No(बीट सं.) : 06
   (b) Address(पता): F 596 ,DURGA FAKIRI MANDIR ,MAIN KARAWAL NAGAR ROAD ,DELHI
   (c) In case, Outside the limit of the Police Station (यदि थाना सीमा के बाहर है):
       Name of P.S.(थाना का नाम):   District(जिला):

6. Complainant / Informant (शिकायतकर्ता/सूचनाकर्ता):
   (a)Name(नाम): RAVI SHARMA (S/O) SH SHIV DAYAL SHARMA
   (b)Date/Year of Birth (जन्म तिथि /वर्ष): 1986   Nationality (राष्ट्रीयता): INDIA
   (c)Passport No.(पासपोर्ट सं.):   Date of Issue (जारी करने की तिथि):   Place of Issue (जारी करने का स्थान):
   (d)Occupation (व्यवसाय):
   (e)Address(पता): H NO 153, SABOLI LONI, GHAZIABAD, UTTAR PRADESH, INDIA.

7. Details of Known/Suspect/Unknown accused with full particulars(attach separate sheet if necessary)(ज्ञात/ संदिग्ध /अज्ञात अभियुक्त का का पूरे विवरण सहित वर्णन):

8. Reason for delay in reporting by the complainant/informant (शिकायतकर्ता / सूचनाकर्ता द्वारा रिपोर्ट देरी से दर्ज कराने के कारण):
   NO DELAY

9. Particulars of the properties stolen/involved (attach separate sheet if necessary):
   Sl.No. (क्र.सं.) Property Type(Description)   Est. Value(Rs.)(मूल्य (रु में))

District : NORTH EAST   P.S: KHAJURIKHAS   Year: 2020   FIR No: 0121   Date: 28/2/2020

10. Total value of property stolen (चोरी हुई सम्पत्ति का कुल मूल्य):

11. Inquest Report / U.D. Case No., if any (मृत्यु समीक्षा रिपोर्ट / यू.डी.केस नं., यदि कोई हो):

12. F.I.R. Contents (attach separate sheet, if required)(प्रथम सूचना रिपोर्ट हम):

सेवा में श्रीमान एस० एच० ओ० साहब थाना खजूरी खास टिम्मी निवेदन इस प्रकार है कि मैं रवि शर्मा S/O श्री शिव ट्यान शर्मा मकान न०-153 सखोली लोनी गाजियाबाद का रहने वाला हूं जो कि मैं श्री दुर्गा फकीरी मन्दिर मैन करावल नगर रोड F 596 में पुजारी के रूप में कार्यरत हूं दिनांक 24/2/2020 को समय करीब टोपहर 2:30 बजे से तीन बजे के आस पास चाँट बाग पुलिया कि तरफ से काफी भीड भजनपुरा चौक तक जमा हो गयी और थोड़ी देर में ही भीड ने पत्थराव शुरू कर दिया और कुछ लोगों ने मन्दिर पर भी पत्थराव किया जिसकी वजह से मन्दिर के मैन गेट का बोर्ड व तीन कैमरों व फर्स्ट फ्लोर पर भी पत्थराव किया जिससे बोर्ड व तीन कैमरे जो बाहर की तरफ लगे थे तोड़ दिये वह कैमरे खराब हो गये व एक कैमरा नही मिला इसीलिए मेरी शिकायत पर उचित कानूनी कार्यवाही की जाये आज दिनांक 28/2/2020 को हमने मन्दिर टोबारा पूजा पाठ के लिये खोल दिया है और आज ही आपको शिकायत दी है थन्यवाद SD HINDI रवि शर्मा S/O श्री शिव ट्यान शर्मा मकान न०-153 सखोली लोनी गाजियाबाद यू० पी० PH-8279280466 28/2/2020 श्रीमान डूपूटी ऑफिसर साहब सरकार निवेदन है कि आज दिनांक 28/2/2020 को HC Rahul No 563/NE बीट गस्त में मौजूद था जो मैं करावल नगर रोड पर F Block में दुर्गा फकीरी मन्दिर के पूजारी ने अपनी एक लिखित शिकायत HC Rahul No 563/NEको दी, वह शिकायत HC Rahul No 563/NEने मन ASIको दी जो थाना हुजा में काफी सारी PCR काल व शिकायत वाबत दंगा झगड़ा, आगजनी व लोड़ पोड़ की घटनाओं के विषय में थाना हुजा में टंगा होने के वाबत कार्यवाही की जा रही है। CAA/NRC के विरोध व समर्थन में चल रहे प्रदर्शन में उप भीड़ ने मन्दिर में पत्थराव व तोड़फोड़ करके नुकसान पहुँचाया लिहाजा हालात से शिकायत से अपराध U/S 147/148/149/427/34 IPC & 03/04 PDPP Act का सरजद होना पाया जाता है लिहाजा तहरीर हुजा बनर्द कायमी मुकद्दमा दर पेश है , मुकद्दमा दर्ज करके No. मुकद्दमा से इत्तला दी जावे मन ASI मशकूफ बालफतीरा हूं लतारीख व वक बकुआ Dt 24.02.20 from 2:30 PM to 3:00PM, घटना स्थल F 596 दुर्गा फकीरी मन्दिर मैन करावल नगर रोड टिम्मी तहरीर पेश करने का समय व दिनांक 28.02.20 at 5:55 PM SD ASI Jamshed Ali No 389/NE PS बजूरी खास Dated 28.02.20 कार्यवाही चुनिस इस समय लिखा है कि एक लेख हिन्दी लिखित ASI JAMSHED ALI No 389/NE व्यान रवि शर्मा S/O श्री शिवट्यान शर्मा द्वारा मुझ SI/DO को थाना मिलने पर प्रथम सूचना संख्या 122/20 U/S 147/148/149/427/34 IPC & 03/04 PDPP Act का CCTNS OPPT W/Ct Himani No 2520/NE द्वारा COMPUTERIZED कराया गयर और COMPUTERIZED COPY OF FIR व मून शिकायतपत्र का हुक्म जनाब SHO साहब ASI Jamshed Ali no.389/NE साहब के ह्वाले की गई जो आगे की विवेचना अमल में लायेगा । व अन्य नकल प्रति डाक के द्वारा उच्च अधिकारीयो की सेवा में प्रस्तुत होंगे CHECKED BY SI/DO

13. Action Taken: Since the above information reveals commission of offence(s) u/s as mentioned at item No. 2: (की गयी कार्यवाही: चूंकि उपरोक्त जानकारी से पता चलता है कि किया गया अपराध मद म.2.में उल्लेख धारा के तहत है):

(i) Registered the case and took up the Investigation: OR (या)
(प्रकरण दर्ज किया गया और जांच के लिए लिया गया):

(ii) Directed (Name of the I.O.)(जांच अधिकारी का नाम): JAMSHED ALI   Rank (पद): ASST. SI (ASSISTANT SUB-INSPECTOR)

No.(सं.): 28010714   to take up the investigation (को जांच अपने वाह में लेने के लिए निर्देश दिया गया) OR(या)

(iii) Refused investigation due to(जांच के लिए):   OR (के कारण इंकार किया या)

(iv) Transferred to P.S(name)(थाना):   District(जिला):
on point of jurisdiction (जो क्षेत्राधिकार के कारण हस्तांतरित)

F.I.R read over to the complainant/informant, admitted to be correctly recorded and a copy given to the complainant/informant, free of cost : (शिकायतकर्ता / सूचनाकर्ता को प्राथमिकी पढ़ कर सुनाई गयी, सही दर्ज हुई माना और एक कॉपी निःशुल्क शिकायतकर्ता को दी गयी):

R.O.A.C.(आर.ओ.ए.सी.):

14. Signature / Thumb impression of the Complainant / Informant: (शिकायतकर्ता / सूचनाकर्ता के हस्ताक्षर / अंगूठे का निशान):

        Signature of Officer
        Name(नाम): CHANDER PAL SINGH
        Rank (पद): SI (SUB-INSPECTOR)
        No.(सं.): 28824101

15. Date and Time of despatch to the court: (अदालत में प्रेषण की दिनांक और समय):

FIRST INFORMATION REPORT
(Under Section 154 Cr.P.C.)

(धारा 154 दंड प्रक्रिया संहिता के तहत)

1. District (जिला): NORTH EAST   P.S.(थाना): DAYAL PUR   Year(वर्ष): 2020   FIR No(प्र.सू.रि.स.): 0090   Date : 02/03/2020

2. Act(s)(अधिनियम):   Section(s)(धारा(एँ)):

   -   IPC 1860   147/148/149/436

   -   PREV. OF DAMAGE TO PUBLIC PROPERTY ACT.   3
      1984

3. Occurrence of Offence (अपराध की घटना):

   (a) Day(दिन):   Date From(दिनांक से):   Date To(दिनांक तक):

     Time Period (समय अवधि):   Time From (समय से):   Time To (समय तक):

   (b)Information received at P.S.(थाना जहाँ सूचना प्राप्त हुई):   Date(दिनांक):   02/03/2020   Time (समय): 19:20 hrs

   (c) General Diary Reference (रोजनामचा संदर्भ):   Entry No.(प्रविष्टि सं.): 112A   Date/Time(दिनांक/समय): 02/03/2020 19:20

4. Type of Information (सूचना का प्रकार):   Written

5. Place of Occurrence (घटनास्थल):

   (a) Direction and Distance from P.S (थाना से दूरी और दिशा): N/A , 00   Km(s)   Beat No(बीट सं.) :   05

   (b) Address(पता): MUNGA NAGAR GALI NO. 5 DELHI

   (c) In case, Outside the limit of the Police Station (यदि थाना सीमा के बाहर है):

     Name of P.S(थाना का नाम):   District(जिला):

6. Complainant / Informant (शिकायतकर्ता/सूचनाकर्ता):

   (a) Name(नाम): SHIV CHARAN MEENA

   (b) Date/Year of Birth (जन्म तिथि /वर्ष): 06/01/1985   Nationality (राष्ट्रीयता):   INDIA

   (c) Passport No.(पासपोर्ट सं.):   Date of Issue (जारी करने की तिथि):   Place of Issue (जारी करने का स्थान):

   (d) Occupation (व्यवसाय):

   (e) Address(पता):   DELHI, DAYAL PUR, NORTH EAST, DELHI, INDIA, 9582974879.

7. Details of Known/Suspect/Unknown accused with full particulars(attach separate sheet if necessary)(ज्ञात संदिग्ध /अज्ञात अभियुक्त का का पूरे विवरण सहित वर्णन):

8. Reason for delay in reporting by the complainant/informant (शिकायतकर्ता / सूचनाकर्ता द्वारा रिपोर्ट देरी से दर्ज करने के कारण):
NO DELAY

9. Particulars of the properties stolen/involved (attach separate sheet if necessary):

   Sl.No. (क्र.सं.) Property Type(Description)   Est. Value(Rs.)(मूल्य (रु में))

District · NORTH EAST   P.S: DAYAL PUR   Year: 2020   FIR No: 0090   Date: 03/03/2020

10. Total value of property stolen (चोरी हुई सम्पत्ति का कुल मूल्य):

11. Inquest Report / U.D. Case No., if any (मृत्यु जांच रिपोर्ट / यू.डी. प्रकरण न., यदि कोई हो):

12. F.I.R. Contents (attach separate sheet, if required)(प्रथम सूचना रिपोर्ट तथ्य):

District NORTH EAST (DELHI) PS DAYAL PUR GD NO. 030A Date 25/02/2020 TIME:02:42:12 Entry Made For Rank / Name / PIS No. of Police Officer SUB-INSPECTOR / NARESH KUMAR/ 28820939 GD Type(s): PCR CALL GD Subject: इत्तला आमद इत्तला PCR CALL GD BRIEF: इस समय टर्न है कि B-54 ने बजरिये टेली फोन इत्तला दी कि MUNGA NAGAR MANDIR ME तोड़ फोड़ हुयू आमद इत्तला PCR CALLटर्न CCTNS कलके बराय मुनासिफ कार्यवाही SI SHIV CHARAN साहब को बजरिये फोन बतलायी गयी। जो मुनासिफ कार्यवाही अमल में लायेंगे SI/DO Signature SUB-INSPECTOR / NARESH KUMAR/ 28820939 NOTE: COMPUTER COPY श्रीमान DUTY OFFICER साहब थाना DAYALPUR निवेदन है कि दिनाक 25/02/2020 को इनका थाना एरिया में CAA के समर्थन और विरोध में दंगा फसाद झगड़ा की घटनायें हो रही थी और मन SI की झमरजनी ड्यूटी थी जो DD NO. 30A बराये ट्रायफक मन SI को मिली थी जिसपर मन SI PCR CALL में दिए गए घटना स्थल के पास पहुंचा जहां करीब 1500/1600 लोग लाठी डन्डे व पत्थरों से लैस होकर CAA के विरोध में समर्थन में प्रदर्शन कर रहे थे जो इलाके में अतिरिक्त सुरक्षा बल भी तैनात किया हुआ था, जहां SHO dayalpur साहब भी मय स्टाफ LAW & ORDER DUTY कर रहे थे जो भीड़ को उग देखकर जनाब SHO साहब ने जमाव को गैरकानूनी करार देते हुए मौका से तितर बितर होने का आदेश दिया परन्तु भीड़ पर इस बात का कोई असर नहीं हुआ और भीड़ एकदम उग होकर पुलिस बल पर पथराव करने लगी और आस पास वाहनों को तोड़ना शुरू कर दिया और MUNGA NAGAR में GALI NO. 5 में बने शिव mandir को भी हन्डों व पत्थरों से तोड़ना शुरू कर दिया, जो पुलिस ने भीड़ को काबू करने के लिए हल्का बल प्रयोग किया, जो हर तरफ अफरा तफरी का माहौल बना हुआ था चारों तरफ आग जनी हो रही थी जो मन SI भी पुलिस बल के साथ आम नागरिकों के जान-माल और सरकारी सम्पति में लगा रहा। जो मन SI को किसी पब्लिक वालों ने आज तक घटना की बाबत न नुकसान की बाबत अपना कोई ब्यान टर्न नहीं कराया । लिहाजा नकल रपट पुस्त हना को तहरीर मानते हुए और हालात के अनुसार जुर्म U/S 147/148/149/436 IPC & 3 PDPP ACT का होना पाया जाता है लिहाजा लेख तैयार करके पेश है। मुकदमा टर्न सिया जाए। मुकदमा टर्न करके नम्बर मुकदमा से इत्तला दी जाये और तफतीश खुद मन SI के हवाले की जाये तारीख व वक्त घटना:- 25/02/2020 AT नामालूमा घटना स्थल- MUNGA NAGAR GALI NO. 5 DELHI. ता० वक पेशगी लिखित लेख:- 02/3/20 AT HRS SD/- ENGLISH SI SHIV CHARAN MEENA D-4238 PS DAYAL PUR DELHI 2/3/20 पुलिस कार्यवाही इस समय एक शिकायत हिन्दी लिखित SI SHIV CHARAN साहब के द्वारा लिखित लेख मुझे ASI/DO ने प्राप्त हुई लेख की प्रति पर मै ASI/DO ने FIR NO 90/2020, U/S 147/148/149/436 IPC & 3 PDPP ACT को CCTNS Operator द्वारा Computer में Feed कराकर असल लेख व FIR की Computerized Copy SI SHIV CHARAN साहब के हवाले की जा रही है जो आईन्दा तफतीश अमल में लायेंगे व अन्य नकल प्रतिया डाक के माध्यम से उच्च अधिकारियों कि सेवा में प्रेषित होंगे ASI/DO.

13. Action Taken Since the above information reveals commission of offence(s) u/s as mentioned at Item No. 2: (की गयी कार्यवाही: चूंकि उपरोक्त जानकारी से पता चलता है कि किया गया अपराध मद सं.2 में उल्लेख क धारा के तहत है):

   (i)Registered the case and took up the investigation: OR (याा
     (प्रकरण दर्ज किया गया और जांच के लिए लिया गया):

   (ii)Directed (Name of the I.O.)(जांच अधिकारी का नाम):   SHIV CHARAN MEENA   Rank (पद):
                                                                           SI (SUB-INSPECTOR)
   No(सं.): 28070137   to take up the investigation (को जांच अपने साथ में लेने के लिए निर्देश दिया गया) OR(या)
   (iii)Refused investigation due to(जांच के लिए):   OR (के कारण इंकार किया गया)
   (iv) Transferred to P.S(name)(थाना):   District(जिला):
     on point of jurisdiction (को क्षेत्राधिकार के कारण इस्तांतरित):

F.I.R. read over to the complainant/informant,admitted to be correctly recorded and a copy given to the complainant/informant, free of cost : (शिकायतकर्ता / सूचनाकर्ता को वाचनिक पढ़ कर सुनाई गयी, सही दर्ज हुई माना और एक प्रति निःशुल्क शिकायतकर्ता को दी गयी) :

R.O.A.C.(आर.ओ.ए.सी.):

2

FIRST INFORMATION REPORT
(Under Section 154 Cr.P.C.)

(धारा 154 दुं प्रक्रिया संहिता के तहत)

1. District (जिला):NORTH EAST   P.S.(थाना): DAYAL PUR   Year(वर्ष): 2020   FIR No(प्र.सू.रि.सं.):0134   Date : 05/03/2020

2. Act(s)(अधिनियम):
   - IPC 1860
   Section(s)(धारा(एँ)):
   147/148/149/436/455/1208/34

3. Occurrence of Offence (अपराध की घटना):
   (a) Day(दिन):   Date From(दिनांक से):   Date To(दिनांक तक):
   Time Period (समय अवधि):   Time From (समय से):   Time To (समय तक):
   (b)Information received at P.S.(थाना जहां सूचना प्राप्त हुई):   Date(दिनांक): 05/03/2020   Time (समय): 18:13 hrs
   (c)General Diary Reference (रोजनामचा संदर्भ):   Entry No.(प्रविष्टि सं.): 04DA   Date/Time(दिनांक का/समय): 05/03/2020 18:13

4. Type of Information (सूचना का प्रकार):   Written

5. Place of Occurrence (घटनास्थल):
   (a) Direction and Distance from P.S (थाना से दूरी और दिशा): _   Beat No(बीट सं.) : 0
   (b) Address(पता): _D.R.P.CONVENT SCHOOL ,BABU NAGAR SHIV VIHAR TIRAHA ,MAIN ROAD BRIJPURI KARAWAL NGR
   (c) In case, Outside the limit of the Police Station (यदि थाना सीमा के बाहर है):
   Name of P.S(थाना का नाम):   District(जिला):

6. Complainant / Informant (शिकायतकर्ता/सूचनाकर्ता):
   (a)Name(नाम): YATENDRA SHARMA (S/O) LATE SH ROOP CHAND SHARMA
   (b)Date/Year of Birth (जन्म तिथि /वर्ष): 1975   Nationality (राष्ट्रीयता):   INDIA
   (c)Passport No.(पासपोर्ट सं.):   Date of Issue (जारी करने की तिथि):   Place of Issue (जारी करने का स्थान):
   (d)Occupation (व्यवसाय):
   (e)Address(पता):   C-9/2, YAMUNA VIHAR DELHI-53, DAYAL PUR, NORTH EAST, DELHI, INDIA, 9312716710,

7. Details of Known/Suspect/Unknown accused with full particulars(attach separate sheet if necessary)(ज्ञात/संदिग्ध /अज्ञात अभियुक्त का का पूरे विवरण सहित वर्णन):

8. Reason for delay in reporting by the complainant/informant (शिकायतकर्ता / सूचनाकर्ता द्वारा रिपोर्ट देरी से दर्ज कराने के कारण):
   NO DELAY

9. Particulars of the properties stolen/involved (attach separate sheet if necessary):
   Sr.No. (क्र.सं.) Property Type(Description)   Est. Value(Rs.)(मूल्य (रु में))

10. Total value of property stolen (चोरी हुई सम्पत्ति का मूल कुल मूल्य):

11. Inquest Report / U.D. Case No., if any (मृत्यु संबंधित रिपोर्ट / यू.डी. प्रकरण सं., यदि कोई हो):

1

District : NORTH EAST   P.S : DAYAL PUR   Year: 2020   FIR No: 039   Date: 05/03/2020

12.F.I.R. Contents (attach separate sheet, if required)(उक्त सूचना रिपोर्ट सत्तः):

D.R.P.CONVENT SEC.SCHOOL RECOGNISED & AFFILIATED TO C.B.S.E Up to X Class Vide No. DDE/NE/(9054)2001, School ID No. 1104393, Babu Nagar, Shiv Vihar Tiraha, Main road Brijpuri-Karawal Nagar-Delhi-94. E-mail- drpgroupofschools@gmail.com Phone No. 82871710710 Website-www.drprcs.comS.No -DRP/SL /20 dated 28.02.2020 SHO DAYALPUR Date 26/02/2020 To.The SHO PS Dayalpur Delhi Dated 28/02/2020 SUB- Regarding the information for lodge the FIR Respected Sir It is submitted as under That I Yatendra Sharma Manager of DRP Convent Secondary School, Babu Nagar, Near Shiv Vihar Tiraha, Delhi-94 wants to inform you that on 24/02/2020 timing around 3:00pm some peoples attacked my above said school with a conspiracy to damages at the level of destroy school building and burn it in fire after the rob. It is further stated that on 24/02/2020 same peoples came down and attacked after falling the rope from the neighbour school roof with the help of rope and some peoples broken the main gate and official block gate and entered inside the school started the assault with the guard of school and his family and they burned the guard quarter and try to kill the guard and his family they were having large number of weapons in the hand of above said assailants were outing a slogans "nara e takdir allah huakbar" and they were shouting that "na hum kissi hindu ko chodengo na uski kisi property ko chodengo That on 24/02/2020 firstly all valuable items was rob from the school like as computers, laptops, Printers Amplifiers, Sound Systems, and many more valuables items the list of robed brems attached here with this information That on the same day they started to broken the school and then after they started the burning all the official and academics blocks which includes reception Manager room. Principal Room Examination Control room, NIOS coordinator room, Record room, Science Lab, Computer lab. Library and all class rooms. All furniture in which all the records are broken the list of concerned documents and items are attached here with from 1998 to till 29/02/2020 . Therefore I request to you kindly lodge a fir as soon as possible in the interest of justice. Thanking you Yours Truly Applicant Yatender Sharma S/o late sh Roop Chand Sharma R/o C-9/2 Yamuna Vihar, Delhi-110053 Manager of DRP Convent Sec. School (M) 9312710710, 9911710710. DO to register a case U/S 147/148/149/436/455/120B/34 IPC and handover investigation to SI RAJEEV Sd/- English Insp. Tarkeshwar Singh PS DAYALPUR 5/3/2020एक शिकायतपत्र ENGLISH TYPE शिकायतपत्र INSP SHO/DAYALPUR साहब के द्वारा शिकायतपत्र मुझे HC /DO ने प्राप्त हुई शिकायत पत्र कि प्राप्ति पर मैं HC /DO ने FIR U/s 147/148/149/436/455/120B/34 IPC को CCTNS Operator द्वारा Computer में feed कराकर असल लेख व FIR कि Computerized Copy SI RAJIV साहब के हवाले की जा रही है। जो बाहुबली जनाब SHO साहब माईन्टा तफ्तीश असल में लायेंगे व अन्य नकल प्रतियाँ डाक के माध्यम से उच्च अधिकारियों की सेवा में प्रेषित होगी। HC/DO

13.Action Taken: Since the above information reveals commission of offence(s) u/s as mentioned at item No. 2:
(की गयी कार्यवाही: चूंकि उपरोक्त जानकारी से पता चलता है कि किया गया अपराध मद सं 2.में उल्लेख धारा के तहत है):

(i) Registered the case and took up the investigation: OR (या)
(प्रकरण दर्ज किया गया और जांच के लिए लिया गया);

(ii) Directed (Name of the I.O.)(जांच अधिकारी का नाम): RAJIV KUMAR   Rank (पद):
                                                        SI (SUB-INSPECTOR)

No(सं.): 16140324   to take up the investigation (को जांच आपने हाथ में लेने के लिए निर्देश दिया गया) OR(या)
(iii)Refused investigation due to(जांच के लिए):   OR (से कारण इंकार किया गया)
(iv)Transferred to P.S(name)(थाना):   District(जिला):
on point of jurisdiction (को क्षेत्राधिकार के कारण हस्तांतरित)

F.I.R read over to the complainant/informant,admitted to be correctly recorded and a copy given to the complainant/informant free of cost : (शिकायतकर्ता / मुखबिरकर्ता को पढ़मिली पढ़ कर सुनाई गयी, सही दर्ज हुई माना और एक कॉपी निःशुल्क शिकायतकर्ता को दी गयी) :

R.O.A.C.(आर.ओ.ए.सी.):

14.Signature / Thumb Impression   Signature of Officer
of the Complainant / Informant:
(शिकायतकर्ता / मुखबिरकर्ता के हस्ताक्षर / अंगूठे का निशान):   Name(नाम): BRIHAM SINGH
                                             Rank (पद): HC (HEAD CONSTABLE)
                                             No.(सं.): 28850288

15.Date and Time of despatch to the court:
(अदालत में प्रेषण की दिनांक और समय):

FIRST INFORMATION REPORT

(Under Section 154 Cr.P.C.)

(धारा 154 दंड प्रकिया सहिता के तहत)

1. District (जिला):NORTH EAST   P.S.(थाना): DAYAL PUR   Year(वर्ष): 2020 FIR No(प्र.सू.रि.सं.):0137   Date :05/03/2020

2. Act(s)(अधिनियम):

- IPC 1860   Section(s)(धारा(एँ)):

                147/148/149/436/427/34

3. Occurrence of Offence (अपराध की घटना):
   - (a) Day(दिन):   MONDAY   Date From(दिनांक से): 24/02/2020   Date To(दिनांक तक): 24/02/2020
   - Time Period (समय अवधि):   Time From (समय से): 19:00 hrs   Time To (समय तक): 19:00 hrs
   - (b) Information received at P.S.(थाना जहाँ सूचना प्राप्त हुई):   Date(दिनांक): 05/03/2020   Time (समय): 22:33 hrs
   - (c) General Diary Reference (रोजनामचा संदर्भ):   Entry No.(प्रविष्टि सं.): 047A Date/Time(दिनांक/समय):05/03/2020 22:33

4. Type of Information (सूचना का प्रकार): Written

5. Place of Occurrence (घटनास्थल):
   - (a) Direction and Distance from P.S (थाना से दूरी और दिशा): NORTH-WEST , 3 Km(s)   Beat No(बीट सं.) : 05
   - (b) Address(पता): ,RAJDHANI PUBLIC SR.SEC. ,SCHOOL A-1, BABU NAGAR, SHIV VIHAR DELHI
   - (c) In case, Outside the limit of the Police Station (यदि थाना सीमा के बाहर हैं):
   - Name of P.S(थाना का नाम):   District(जिला):

6. Complainant / Informant (शिकायतकर्ता/सूचनाकर्ता):
   - (a) Name(नाम): FAISAL FAROOQ (S/O) SH FAROOQ AHMAD NAWAB
   - (b) Date/Year of Birth (जन्म तिथि /वर्ष): 1982   Nationality (राष्ट्रीयता):   INDIA
   - (c) Passport No.(पासपोर्ट सं.):   Date of Issue (जारी करने की तिथि):   Place of Issue (जारी करने का स्थान):
   - (d) Occupation (व्यवसाय):
   - (e) Address(पता): RAJDHANI PUBLIC SR. SEC. SCHOOL, A-1, BABU NAGAR SHIV VIHAR, DELHI -94,
   - DAYAL PUR, NORTH EAST, DELHI, INDIA,

7. Details of Known/Suspect/Unknown accused with full particulars(attach separate sheet if necessary)(ज्ञात/ संदिग्ध / अज्ञात अभियुक्त का का पूरे विवरण सहित वर्णन):

8. Reason for delay in reporting by the complainant/informant (शिकायतकर्ता / सूचनाकर्ता द्वारा रिपोर्ट देरी से दर्ज कराने के कारण):
   NO DELAY

9. Particulars of the properties stolen/involved (attach separate sheet if necessary):

   Sl.No. (क्र.सं.) Property Type(Description)   Est. Value(Rs.)(अनुमा (र में))

10. Total value of property stolen (चोरी हुई सम्पति का कुल मूल्य):

11. Inquest Report / U.D. Case No., if any (मृत्यु समीक्षा रिपोर्ट / यू.डी.प्रकरण न., यदि कोई हो):

District : NORTH EAST	P.S: DAYAL PUR	Year: 2020	FIR No: 138	Date: 01/03/2020

12. F.I.R. Contents (attach separate sheet, if required)(इस सूचना रिपोर्ट तथ्य):

DD.NO.46B, Dated -27/2/2020 Dy. No. 19, Dated -2/3/2020 SHO PS-DAYAL PUR श्रीमान SHO साहब थाना ट्यालनपुर N/E Distt. माननीय निवेदन इस प्रकार है मैं फैसल फारूक पुत्र श्री फारूक अहमद नवाब, राजधानी पब्लिक सि. से०. स्कूल का सचिव हूँ दिनांक 24/2/2020 को करीब 2 बजे दिन स्कूल की छुट्टी के पश्चात मैं स्कूल बंद करके वहाँ मौजूद दो स्कूल गार्डों जिनके नाम श्री मनोज एवं राजकुमार के हवाले करके अपने घर आया या समय करीब 7-8 बजे मनोज ने फोन करके मुझे बताया कि तकरीबन 300-400 दंगाईयो ने स्कूल का गेट तोड़कर स्कूल पर कब्जा कर लिया है और हमें यह कहा है कि जिन्दा रहना चाहता हो तो भाग जा। आज दिनांक 27/2/2020 को जब मैं स्कूल पहुँचा तो मैंने देखा कि स्कूल पूरी तरह बर्बाद किया जा चुका है। स्कूल का सारा रिकार्ड जला दिया गया है। Computer Lab, Scince Lab, Library को लूट दिया गया है। Book में आग लगा दी गई है। सारा फर्नीचर पूरी तरह नष्ट कर दिया गया है। मैं सारे हालात को देखकर बहुत डर गया हूँ। मुझे अपनी जान का खतरा है। मैं इस हट तक डर गया हूँ कि मेरा मन जिन्दा रहने का नहीं है अत: आपसे निवेदन है कि मेरी शिकायत दर्ज कि जाये। मुनासिब कार्यवाही की जाए। स्कूल को Security Provide कराई जाए। स्कूल में पढ़ने वाले बच्चो की SECURITY को यकीनी बनाया जाए। धन्यवाद Sd English Faisal Farooq School Address- Rajdhani Public Sr. Sec.Schools A-1, Babu Nagar Shiv Vihar Delhi-94 9811313786 Do to register a case u/s 147/148/149/436/427/34 IPC and hand over investigation to SI SHIV CHARAN SHO/P.S. DAYAL PUR 5/3/20 कार्यवाही पुलिस अज थाना एम शिकायत हिन्दी TYPE शिकायतपत्र INSP. SHO/DAYALPUR साहब के द्वारा शिकायतपत्र मुझ HC/DO को प्राप्त हुई। शिकायत पत्र कि प्रति पर मैं HC/DO ने FIR NO.137/2020, U/s 147/148/149/436/427/34 IPC का CCTNS Operator द्वारा Computer में feed कराकर असल लेख व FIR कि Computerized Copy SI SHIV CHARAN साहब के हवाले की जा रही है। जो माहतवम जनाब SHO साहब आईन्दा तफ्तीश अमल में लायेंगे व अन्य नकल प्रतियाँ डाक के माध्यम से उच्च अधिकारियों की सेवा में प्रेषित होंगी। HC/DO

13. Action Taken Since the above information reveals commission of offence(s) u/s as mentioned at Item No. 2:
(की गयी कार्यवाही: भूंकि उपरोक्त जानकारी से पता चलता है कि किसी तरह अपराध बट स.2.में उल्लेख द्वारा के तहत है):

                                                 OR (या)

  (i) Registered the case and took up the investigation:
  (पंजरन दर्ज किया गया और जांच के लिए लिया गया):
  (ii) Directed (Name of the I.O.)(जांच अधिकारी का नाम): SHIV CHARAN MEENA

                                                      Rank (पद):
                                                      SI (SUB-INSPECTOR)

  No(सं.): 28070137   to take up the investigation (को जांच आपरे जांच में लेने के लिए निर्देश दिया गया) OR(या)

                                                      OR (के कारण इकार किया गा)

  (iii) Refused investigation due to(जांच के लिए):

  (iv) Transferred to P.S(name)(थाना):   District(जिला):
      on point of jurisdiction (को क्षेत्राधिकार के कारण हस्तांतरित)

F.I.R. read over to the complainant/informant, admitted to be correctly recorded and a copy given to the complainant/informant, free of cost : (शिकायतकर्ता / सूचनाकर्ता को शिकायती पढ़ कर सुनाई गयी, सही दर्ज हुई माना और एक कॉपी निशुल्क शिकायतकर्ता को दी गयी) :

R.O.A.C.(आर.ओ.ए.सी.):

GARUDA PRAKASHAN BOOKS

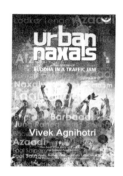

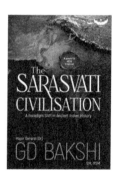

GARUDA PRAKASHAN BOOKS

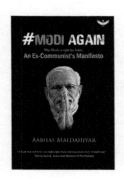

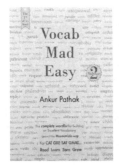

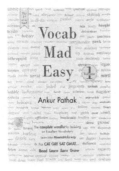

गरुड

Register:

Please register your book purchase at **grpr.in/register** to stay in touch and get informed about future books!

To order:

www.garudabooks.com

Follow us:

WEBSITE   : **www.garudabooks.com**

FACEBOOK   : **www.facebook.com/garudaprakashan/**

TWITTER   : **@garudaprakashan**

INSTAGRAM : **@garudabooks**

YOUTUBE   : **/garudabooks**

Contact:

EMAIL   : **contact@garudabooks.com**

International queries:

EMAIL   : **international@garudabooks.com**

ABOUT THE AUTHORS

Monika Arora is a senior advocate in the Delhi High Court and the Supreme Court of India and the Convener of the Group of Intellectuals and Academicians (GIA). She is the standing counsel for Jawaharlal Nehru University and has represented JNU in important matters in court. She has been a counsel for various ministries including the Home ministry, Finance ministry, External affair ministry and the ministry of Human Resource and Development. She has fought thousands of cases in various courts. She is a powerful orator and has participated in various seminars/ awareness campaigns on Uniform Civil Code and ending discrimination against women. She has been fighting for women's right to equality, freedom and dignity.

Sonali Chitalkar is Assistant Professor, Department of Political Science at Miranda House, University of Delhi. Her area of Specialization is International Relations with a focus on Conflict Resolution. She has been working on the State of Jammu and Kashmir as a part of peace facilitation. She is currently working on the framework of an Indic Theory of Gender as a part of her interest in Decolonisation of the Indian mind and Indigenous Political Theory.

Dr. Prerna Malhotra teaches English at Ram Lal Anand College, Delhi University. She is the author of several books and is a prolific speaker and social influencer. She has worked extensively in Bastar and is a passionate voice for the rights of tribals of Bastar and against their brutalization by Urban Naxals.

All three authors are residents of Delhi.

Printed in Great Britain
by Amazon